Facilities Planning and Maintenance

For Private-Independent Schools

SECOND EDITION

ism Publications

Facilities Planning and Maintenance for Private-Independent Schools

Second Edition

Independent School Management
1316 North Union Street
Wilmington, DE 19806
PHONE 302-656-4944 • FAX 302-656-0647
WEB isminc.com/bookstore • EMAIL bookstore@isminc.com

All rights reserved. No part of this book may be reproduced or transmitted in any form or by any means, electronic or mechanical, including photocopying, scanning, recording, or by any information storage and retrieval system without the permission of Independent School Management, except for brief quotations with attribution.

This book's content is a topical compilation of articles previously published in ISM's advisory letters. The articles have been edited and reformatted specifically for this edition.

Disclaimer: ISM provides management consulting services to private-independent schools. ISM is not a law firm. No service or information provided by ISM should be construed as legal advice. All Web links and references in this book are correct as of the publication date, but may have become inactive or otherwise modified since that time.

Copyright © 2017 by Independent School Management

ISBN-13: 978-1-883627-15-7

Table of Contents

The 21st Century School: Facilities 1
Facility Planning and Future Needs 3
A Checklist for the Comprehensive Long Range Property/Facilities Plan 5
Cost-Effective, Sustainable Building Solutions 7
Replace, Repair, Renew: Why a Facilities Audit Helps 9
The Deferred Maintenance Account 11
Selling PPRRSM to the Board 13
Limited-Area, Moderate-Cost Space Reconfigurations 15
Campus Master Plan Supports Good Decision-Making 17
A Maintenance Plan Extends the Useful Life of Facilities 19
The Role of the Board's Buildings and Grounds Committee 21
Keep Evolving Program Needs on Your Facilities 'Radar' 23
Land: Always Your School's Best Investment 25
Land Acquisition Plans: Context and Action 27
Facilities: When You Run Out of Money 29
The Eight Steps of Facility Planning 31
Facility Design and Strategic Planning 33
Educational Specifications: The Foundation for the Facility of Your Dreams 35
Why Spend Educators' Time Planning Facilities? 39
Construction in Your Future? Watch For Environmental and Zoning Issues 41
Construction Ahead: An Owner's Representative Protects Your Interests 43
Reduce Construction Anxiety for Your School's Neighbors 45
When Does it Make Sense to Hire an Architect? 47
How to Identify the Appropriate Architect for the Job 49
Facilities Projects: Get Organized! 53
Your School's Facilities: Preserve and Enhance Their Unique Character 55
Facilities Rentals Yield Benefits—As Long As You Cover Costs 57
Planning School Grounds for Outdoor Learning 59
Classroom Acoustics and Learning 61
Streamline Your Housekeeping Services 63
Common Restroom Problems and Student Health 67
Your School's Indoor Air Quality: Is It Hazardous? 69
Teams Keep an Eye on Campus Safety 71
Checklist Identifies Steps to Improve Security on Your Campus 73
Establish a 'Key' Policy/Security System 75
Facilities and Faculty Retention 77
Faculty, Facilities, and Technology 79
Facilities Management for the Year-Round School 81

The 21st Century School: Facilities

If you, as School Head or Board President, are thinking of or are in the process of planning new or renovated facilities, ISM recommends that you ask this simple question: *What do we know about the uses and need for this building in five to 10 years?*

The honest answer given the dramatic changes in the delivery of education that we and many others have been commenting on is that we are not at all sure. However, there are strong hints and emerging practices in school architecture that provide us with a little confidence in thinking about our next projects.

Hint No. 1

In the 20th century, buildings were driven by the needs of the curriculum. This will not be true of the 21st century. Curriculum is being reviewed and changed in public schools as often as every five years in state mandates. Changes in political allegiances are creating the climate for more immediate changes. Both the rate of increase of knowledge and the political climate are invigorating change constantly. In many schools, best practice sees curriculum as an ongoing conversation and ongoing development process rather than as a periodic, fixed event. Faculty are now going online to cocreate curriculum with their colleagues across the world on a daily basis. So we cannot look to curriculum to determine long-term needs, and planning on the basis of curriculum needs today, which is likely to prove very expensive in the long run.

Hint No. 2

In the 20th century, schools met stable requirements in terms of their building and energy codes. The 21st century regulatory environment; concerns about global warming; access to on-site energy sources through, for example, solar, wind, and geothermal; the necessity for preserving micro-ecosystems on school grounds; low impact practices with regard to storm water management and water quality; the move to water conservation; issues around transportation including the potential of electric cars (charging stations); and finally the decentralization of communications, all suggest a highly flexible approach to planning.

Hint No. 3

Ongoing research into the connection between space and place is demonstrating strong correlations between design and student performance. The National Foundation for Educational Research in the United Kingdom is studying the effects of the rebuilding initiative of all of England's 3500 state secondary schools. The first study, carried out during the first rebuild in 2007, found that students felt safer (57%–87%), felt proud of their school (43%–77%), enjoyed going to school (50%–61%). Interestingly, when asked what they found the most important to them at school, the answers were technology, clean toilets, and clean changing rooms. While none of this research is conclusive, it suggests that design matters, and that talking to the prime users—students—is an important 21st century practice.

Hint No. 4

The 20th Century School is a factory model of design with an emphasis on adult command and control. This is symbolized by the double-loaded corridor (fixed and identical classrooms on either side of a central and linear corridor) and the "gross-to-net ratio" concept which considers everything except classroom space to be nonlearning space. Thus corridors, cafeterias, entranceways, etc. are necessities but not integral to learning. The classroom is the central mode of learning with the following assumptions:

– all students are ready to learn the same thing at the same time in the same way from the same person,
– learning is passive,
– one teacher can be all things to 20–30 students simultaneously, and
– learning happens under teacher control.

The 21st Century School, however, may be moving from the classroom unit as the basic building block to the small learning community of 150 students as the main building block. This model, akin to the homeroom in the lower school and the ISM fluid block in the middle school, imagines fluid teaching areas with corridors acting as "learning streets" unifying the various learning centers. In this model, there are few nonlearning spaces (most spaces are multifunctional), and faculty work as learning/teaching teams. These concepts continue the move from an adult-centered environment to a student-centered environment.

Action Steps

With these "hints" in mind, take the following action steps.

1. Ensure that your campus master development plan is up to date.
2. Integrate students into all aspects of planning phases for renovation and building in meaningful ways, seeing them as the primary user and potential leaders in the process.
3. Just as 21st Century Schools begin to treat knowledge as unitary and curriculum as cross-disciplinary, so, too, consider design connections between, for example, music and math, art and science, and humanities. Form ad hoc discussion groups of faculty to consider these connections and report back to the faculty as a whole. Require your designers to meet with such faculty groups.
4. Consider your mission and its implications for design—include learning parameters that are broad and inclusive such as independent study, peer tutoring, team collaboration, lecture, projects, and so on. Create your own list.
5. In your quadrennial strategic planning session preparation, if renovation or building is envisaged, require meaningful conversation about the difference between the 20th century factory model and the 21st century learning community model that has demonstrated practical, mission-appropriate outcomes—integrate student leaders into those discussions.
6. Ensure that any current or future planning incorporates the essential principle of flexibility, i.e., we don't really know. The most important design element for this is the concept that only outside walls should be load-bearing so that interior design can continually be modified as needed.

Finally, private schools may be forced to ally with their local communities both as outreach (meeting joint needs), and connecting to the support base. School as community center is not a new idea. In the 21st century, it may prove to turn our schools from isolated members geographically located in a setting, to an integrated member of the community.

While we don't know what the future holds, we do know that it will not look like the past. Don't plan or build in a way that represents a 20th century model of either building or learning. Look at renovation and new building as an opportunity to move towards a student-centered design process that will optimize mission-appropriate learning.

Facility Planning and Future Needs

Boards and School Heads must keep their eyes on the horizon when planning for an upgrade or adaptation of an existing facility, or designing a new one. What programs and services will private-independent schools need to offer in the next 10 years to remain competitive? How do they influence the planning and design of new—or adaptation of existing—school buildings?

While it is difficult to plan using a "crystal ball" outlook, there are trends that you need to consider. If your planning document calls for significant shifts in program, changes in facilities and services may include:

- expanded use of technology as younger teachers with greater computer literacy than the previous generation of teachers come into classrooms. Students, as well, will come to school as early as kindergarten with basic computer skills under their belts;
- more "hands-on," high-tech multimedia production facilities as the definition of visual and performing arts is expanded to make use of the tools of the 21st century;
- classrooms without walls—interactive learning that can take place anywhere, at any time;
- team teaching and nonchronological age groupings of students;
- distance learning studios to bring specialized teachers to your students (as well as allowing you to serve home-schooled students for a fee);
- use of these same electronic studios to produce parent and community-based learning programs geared to support parents with child rearing;
- athletic facilities to serve an ever-expanding array of sports and other activities, not only for your school community but as a resource (via rental) to your locality;
- the need for increased perimeter and interior security on campus to respond to increasing safety concerns;
- support services and programs shared with schools, colleges and universities, religious institutions, museums, social service agencies, etc. In partnership with your school, these agencies, in turn, could offer your students real-life experiences to facilitate their community service or work-study experience; and
- expanded food-services facilities that are equipped to offer a variety of meal options—not only for your students, but on a fee basis for dual-working parents and senior citizens.

As you build and renovate, strive to make space as flexible as possible. You'll likely use space differently five years from now. Whatever your course, it should be incorporated into a strategic plan. Because most of these ideas require funding, start now to identify and cultivate donors who can help your school fulfill its dreams (and mission). Don't overlook the need to adjust your operating budget to shift or add funds for new initiatives when developing your strategic plan.

Keep these ideas on your "radar" as you think and plan for facilities that will place your school in the forefront—making you more attractive to the next generation of mission-appropriate students. Strategic planning calls for creative thinking, but allows for some "what ifs" as well. What should your school look like in the next 10, 20, or more years? Plan accordingly.

A Checklist for the Comprehensive Long Range Property/Facilities Plan

In the context of the quadrennial strategic planning cycle, Trustees and senior administrators should give careful attention to your "long range property/facilities plan's."

Planners should be aware of the distinction between:

- a campus master plan, which is a mission-driven delineation of the physical characteristics of the future campus; and
- a preventive/deferred maintenance plan, which comprises the annual (usually rotating) sequence of steps taken by an administration to maintain the structural and functional integrity of the current campus.

The campus master plan is not a substitute for a preventive/deferred maintenance plan and should not be created to correct for the failure to attend to the current property and its facilities.

The following checklist (see next page) is divided into two broad categories: (a) campus master (physical) plan, items No. 1 to 11; and (b) land acquisition plan, items No. 12 to 15. Both categories should be considered in developing a comprehensive property/facilities plan.

Next Steps

If you—as School Head, Business Manager, or Board committee member—found yourself checking "no" much of the time, you should reconsider the extent to which your Board is attempting to function as a strategic entity.

If your Board has had a strategic focus for some time, then you should find it easy to integrate property/facilities planning into your strategic planning cycle. Schools with strategic planning events coming up within the next 12 months will be able to incorporate property/facilities planning at that time. Those whose cycles call for strategic planning events more than a year from now may consider placing property/facilities items into the annual Board and/or administrative agenda even though such items do not yet appear in the planning document itself.

Note that items No. 13 and 14 on the checklist—those pertaining to major gifts and real estate monitoring—can be put into place much more rapidly than can a campus master plan. Consider doing so even though such monitoring does not follow the ideal sequence (i.e., master plan development first, so that an assessment of the master plan's specific limitations can be used to drive the analysis of land acquisition needs). The components of the land acquisition plan can be refined as the master plan's implications become evident over time.

Prepare now to incorporate the checklist into your annual agenda-setting and/or your next strategic planning event.

The Comprehensive Long Range Property/Facilities Plan Checklist

1. There is a document—the campus master plan—that delineates the physical characteristics of our campus five years (or more) from today. Yes ❑   No ❑

2. The master plan document is in regular use. Yes ❑   No ❑

3. The master plan is explicitly mission-related (i.e., enhances the school's ability to fulfill its mission). Yes ❑   No ❑

4. The master plan is integrated with ongoing technology planning. Yes ❑   No ❑

5. The master plan is integrated with ongoing curriculum and cocurriculum planning. Yes ❑   No ❑

6. The master plan is integrated with ongoing strategic financial planning. Yes ❑   No ❑

7. The master plan is integrated with ongoing development and major gifts programs. Yes ❑   No ❑

8. The master plan is integrated with ongoing student recruitment/enrollment management programs. Yes ❑   No ❑

9. The master plan is integrated with ongoing public/parent/alumni relations programs. Yes ❑   No ❑

10. The master plan has been produced in a form that makes it readily usable in public or private presentations. Yes ❑   No ❑

11. The master plan has been used as part of an assessment of the school's property requirements and location for the long-term future (i.e., 50–100 years). Yes ❑   No ❑

12. An assessment of the school's property requirements and location for the long-term future has generated a land acquisition plan. *Note:* Unlike the master plan, the land acquisition plan is not necessarily a document; see the following items in the checklist. Yes ❑   No ❑

13. The Board of Trustees' major gifts program systematically incorporates issues of property and location in its cultivation of lead donors. Yes ❑   No ❑

14. The land acquisition plan includes the real estate monitoring function (i.e., the systematic tracking of tendencies or anticipated directions in demographic development, zoning changes, land prices, etc.). Yes ❑   No ❑

15. The land acquisition plan includes the systematic and proactive exploration of land purchase or lease-purchase opportunities in areas implied by the assessment and monitoring processes (see items No. 12 and 14). Yes ❑   No ❑

Cost-Effective, Sustainable Building Solutions

Sustainability is no longer a trend; it is an integral part of conversations about school design and management. Sustainability, green buildings, and high-performance buildings are all part of the conversation—and, although the three terms are used interchangeably, it is helpful to remember that, while green buildings incorporate a number of sustainable ideas, the terms are not synonymous.

Sustainability encompasses the simple principle of taking from the earth only what it can provide indefinitely, thus leaving future generations no less than we have access to ourselves.

In a study for the state of Minnesota, the following statistics were reported as representative of buildings in the United States. The buildings:
– consume about 65% of the total electricity generated in the U.S.;
– use 12% of potable water;
– generate 2.8 lbs/person of construction and demolition waste every day; and
– contribute 30% of total U.S. greenhouse gas emissions.

Considering these statistics, the easiest way for a school to make an impact is to find ways to make its buildings and campus more energy efficient, using building materials that can be recycled. Although many schools want to make the commitment, they often resort to more conventional ideas rather than taking the perceived risks associated with going green. Here are the four most common myths, followed by the refutation.

Myth 1: "Affordability dictates more traditional choices."

In fact, a number of green options are comparable in price and can be more economical than their conventional counterparts when you look at the life cycle of the product.

When designing green, your team needs to look at the life-cycle cost and efficiencies of the systems, as well as health and other benefits. This is a different approach than the common practice of judging building choices merely on the basis of initial cost and then installing cheaper systems (even if it reduces building efficiency).

The return on investment (ROI)—for those who will spend a little more up front—can be great, especially when deciding on green options. See the table below, Sustainable Building Solutions and Return on Investment. ROI should not be calculated only in money, but by the total effect of the product or system, which may include:
– a cleaner, healthier environment;
– spaces that are more conducive to learning;
– buildings that will save a portion of the energy cost each year over conventional design, thus assuring a more positive environmental impact; and
– systems with longer life cycles, requiring less maintenance.

While it is true that green options may cost more than what is typically used, the cost differential is becoming smaller and smaller. Calculating the cost efficiency and other positive variables over a building's life cycle often makes the green decision preferable.

Myth 2: "The promised payback for green products may not be realized for a very long period of time."

Today, many of these systems pay off in a short time, especially with rising energy and oil prices. After the payback years, you'll have buildings that are returning those savings every year, and not wasting electricity, oil, gas, or water.

Myth 3: "It is better to select a familiar solution than use a design or product that may be perceived as untested or unconventional."

There are many new products that have been adequately tested and found to work well.

Sustainable Building Solutions and Return on Investment

Replacement of older light fixtures with new T8 or T5 lamps

Replacement cost for 100 fixtures: $16,000   ROI: $4,000 per year

The payback on replacement cost is in four years. By year five (because of the inflationary cost for electricity), there will be a savings of over $16,000. The superior lighting will create a better learning environment. The new lamps have less or no mercury and are more easily maintained.

Replacement of existing roof with green roof (6,700 sq. ft.)

Replacement cost for existing roof: $105,000

Cost of green roof installation: $60,000

Total roof cost: $165,000   ROI: $600,000

A typical rubber roofing system lasts 15–20 years. This new roof will last two or three times as long because of the green roofing application. The ROI over the life of the new roof (60 years), adjusted for inflation, is approximately $600,000.

This does not include the savings on air-conditioning in the summer or the storm water credit given to the school by the county. The credit would save approximately $30,000 on the next construction project.

Replacement of automatic flush urinals with waterless urinals

Cost of installing five waterless urinals: $4,250   ROI: $1,500 per year

The payback on replacement cost is in three to four years. The savings per unit after that (based on expected savings in reduced water and sewer costs) is approximately $300 per year, not accounting for inflation ($300/yr for each unit X 5 = $1,500/yr).

One example is a product that uses compressed plant stalks to create a material that can be used in place of wood in many situations. Because it is composed of plant material, it can only be used in building areas that are dry and not exposed to water, but is as sturdy and as useful as most wood products.

Your decision to use sustainable products may limit your choices. However, if your campus is committed to being green, you can often find a viable option among the alternate materials available. You may also find that a new sustainable product does not work for every application of the product it is replacing.

Myth 4: "Green products, especially cleaning materials, do not work as well as the current products being used."

Most sustainable products are effective for their purposes.

The green products are also more environmentally friendly and may help to create a healthier environment in your buildings. It is up to the school to decide if this quality is sufficient to warrant purchasing these products, and determine how they fit into a campus sustainability plan.

How green a campus will become is going to be determined by the commitment of the school and its administration, but it is a driving movement few schools can ignore. The only question that every school administration needs to answer is what shade of green their campus will be.

Replace, Repair, Renew: Why a Facilities Audit Helps

Your school should have a master property/facilities plan in place and in use. This planning document, designed to be a part of the strategic planning process that drives the school's growth. The planning document lays out a preventive maintenance schedule for existing buildings and grounds (together with estimated costs and revenue sources), as well as projected new-structures/new-acreage expectations.

A facilities audit will provide much of the data you need to create this schedule, as well as help you design a carefully staged implementation plan. The audit is a precondition for future planning.

Maintenance Issues

Schools often postpone needed maintenance and replacement due to budget constraints. So the first step in the facilities audit is to determine a preventive maintenance schedule that ensures that the physical integrity of your buildings does not deteriorate beyond its current condition. This step identifies the major systems and infrastructures, and the annual maintenance required for each. The actual annual maintenance cost should be reflected on the maintenance line item of the operations budget.

Items that are not an annual expense are accounted for through the Physical Plant Replacement, Repairs, and Special Maintenance (PPRRSM) allocation in the budget. PPRRSM in a maintenance budget will often be a depreciation account; depreciation all too often is an account that is not funded. It is important for the Board to understand that this is not true depreciation (e.g., as the worth of a car depreciates over time), but an actual physical replacement cost for worn-out systems within the building. A prime result of this first step in the facilities audit is placing a real dollar figure into the PPRRSM line of the budget. (When scheduled PPRRSM work is not performed, it is reallocated into a deferred maintenance account.) From a year-to-year standpoint, it does not seem as critical as salaries, utilities, or the mortgage. However, from a strategic point of view, this budget line represents what is needed to maintain the facility.

Over time, the actions needed to maintain the facility can increase to the point where the facility may be unsuitable or even unsafe, and where the amount of money required to address the issues may be overwhelming. To ensure this does not happen, and that the current maintenance is being appropriately funded, include these items in the second step. This step identifies and addresses the deferred maintenance issues. Examples of deferred maintenance might be:

- infrastructure systems that, because they have gone beyond their life cycles, are damaging other systems within the building;
- carpets that are worn;
- walls that need painting;
- roofs that are not able to weather a storm and develop additional leaks year after year;
- playground equipment that does not conform to new regulations;
- windows that have outlived their life span;
- electrical and/or plumbing systems that are no longer efficient; and
- athletic field surfaces that have become unsafe for play.

The resulting list is then turned into a strategic plan (i.e., each item is assigned to a specific year or years over the life of the plan). The plan is submitted through the Building and Grounds Committee to the Finance Committee for inclusion in both the budgeting process and the school's next strategic planning process.

Note that the extent of an audit depends on the time and resources that are available to the Facilities Manager. Determine which questions will provide the most essential information, who will ask those questions, and who will answer them. If the resources are available, other important questions might relate to energy conservation measures and their return on investment. A new building will need less attention than buildings that are 15–30 years old or more. One way to assess the level required (from a strategic Board viewpoint) is to consider the level of "fixes" being required each year compared to preventive work.

Actions to Take

At a minimum, schools should do the following.

- Establish a Building and Grounds Committee as an operations committee to whom the custodian, Business Manager, or Facilities Director—depending on the size of your school —makes regular reports.
- Create an annual report that includes:
  - the results of the annual "walk around" with the fire inspector (a free service);
  - the results of the annual walk around with your insurance agent (a free service); and
  - notes of repairs that are repetitive and thus denote significant issues.

Preferably, schools should also do the following.

- Ask their contracted service vendors to assist in auditing the infrastructures for which they are responsible. Plumbing or HVAC companies may be the most helpful. There may or may not be fees associated with this.
- If new construction is planned, perform a space analysis to look at building use.

As an alternative, schools can bring in a consulting firm to carry out a full facilities audit or utilize a competent Building and Grounds Committee to do the same. The results should include:

- a complete listing of major systems and infrastructures (electrical, plumbing, HVAC, building structures, etc.);
- the life span of the components of each system and structure; and
- the cost of replacement at the end of that life span in today's dollars.

The desired outcome is a facilities plan, laid out on a time line that clarifies how much is needed to maintain the present facilities, how much is required to do "catch-up" (deferred maintenance), and when those funds will be required. Use this plan to:

- reduce deferred maintenance over time;
- improve the safety of the school for the children, which reduces liability;
- educate the Board of Trustees about facility needs;
- provide information that supports the strategic plan; and
- ensure that future building projects are planned in terms of their life-cycle costs, up-front construction costs compared with long-term savings (e.g., in lighting, typically 60% of electrical costs), and the standards that need to be set to ensure excellence in long-term maintenance.

Finally, ensure that construction contractors provide systems lists that include both maintenance schedules and life cycle estimates. This information should then be added to the plan on an ongoing basis.

Carrying out a facilities audit, and then updating it on a regular basis, saves many expensive headaches and enables good financial planning for the future. It also provides the cornerstone for the overall facilities and grounds master plan, helping shape the future of the school's physical environment.

The Deferred Maintenance Account

Your school may have limited or no cash reserves. The Board, Head, and Management Team understand that your buildings are depreciating, and a depreciation line in your school's budget reflects this.

A 1997 report, "A Foundation to Uphold," identified $26 billion of deferred maintenance for institutions of higher education nationally. (This included $6 billion of urgent needs.) While ISM knows of no similar study for private-independent schools, ISM Consultants have visited many schools where a deferred maintenance backlog exists.

ISM has consistently taught the importance of cash reserves equal to 20% of the operating budget, which includes a 5% allocation for Physical Plant Replacement, Repairs, and Special Maintenance (PPRRSM). What does that allocation cover? And what is the difference between depreciation, PPRRSM, deferred maintenance, and general maintenance and repairs? Here are key definitions of these terms.

- **Depreciation:** reflects the use of fixed assets; the assets depreciate in value at a fixed rate (e.g., 2% per annum on foundations and walls); it does not include inflation; it does not include items under a certain price level (e.g., $5,000 or $10,000).
- **General Maintenance and Repairs:** everyday upkeep of buildings and grounds, including items under a certain price level (e.g., $5,000 or $10,000).
- **PPRRSM:** an account that is spent on items over a certain price level (e.g., $5,000 or $10,000), and/or expenditures that occur on a periodic basis (e.g., the replacement of heat pumps every 12 years); this account, funded from tuition, is based on the estimates of expenditures derived through a Master Property/Facilities Plan and a Facility Audit; estimates are inflation adjusted on a "best-guess" basis.
- **Deferred Maintenance:** items from general maintenance and repairs and the PPRRSM account that have not been carried out and need to be addressed in the future.

For many schools, depreciation as a budget line is seen as a noncash (accounting) item that is often written off at the end of the fiscal year to balance the budget. While the immediate effects of this are usually minimal, the long-term impact on the school's ability to sustain safe, healthy, and mission-appropriate facilities can have serious consequences. The effects can be:

– hazardous conditions in and outside of buildings;
– unusable spaces;
– unattractive interiors and exteriors of buildings and grounds;
– missed enrollment goals (the appearance of your facility does not match the expectations of those who visit the campus); and
– poor fiscal management due to increasing inefficiencies in your plant operations.

Unfunded depreciation and deferred maintenance represent a liability, not an asset to your accounts. The fiscal realities can be overwhelming. If you, as Business Manager, find your school in this position, take these steps.

- Ensure that your budget includes three lines: general maintenance, PPRRSM, and deferred maintenance.
- Develop and keep updated your Master Property/Facilities Plan and Facility Audit.
- Make sure your school's needs (as indicated by your data points) are communicated to the School Head, the Buildings and Grounds Committee and, as appropriate, to Board members as part of the quadrennial strategic planning process.
- Take the scheduled tasks that were not performed last year (as laid out in your general maintenance/repair and PPRRSM plan) and ensure that they are reallocated from those accounts into the deferred maintenance account.
- Treat the depreciation line as an accounting line, not a cash line.
- Through your quadrennial strategic planning event, ensure that the PPRRSM part of the cash reserves is both appropriately funded today and into the future on an inflation basis.
- During strategic planning, work to reverse any deferred maintenance needs through an extra infusion of funds.

ISM has consistently taught that you should fund your PPRRSM account with an amount equivalent to 2.5% to 3% of the replacement value of your facilities. This practice has changed, however, and we are now recommending an amount equivalent to 5% to 7%. This may have an impact on the total cash reserves that would be ideal. (The higher 7% is most applicable to schools with deferred maintenance backlogs. A new or young school with newer facilities would use the 5% amount.)

For example, using a 20% calculation I&P Academy, with a total budget of $7 million, would place $1.4 million in its cash reserve. But I&P has a facility valued at $12.5 million. Using the 5% estimate, cash needed for the PPRRSM account is $625,000. So the cash reserve needed at I&P Academy would be:

Operating Reserve (15% of budget): $1,050,000

PPRRSM Reserve (5% of replacement cost): $625,000

Total Ideal Cash Reserve (24% of budget): $1,675,000

The upper end of the range (7%) would come into effect when working with significant deferred maintenance issues. To eliminate that backlog over time, the PPRRSM account would be as much as $875,000. In that case, the cash reserve would be:

Operating Reserve (15% of budget): $1,050,000

PPRRSM Reserve (5% of replacement cost): $875,000

Total Ideal Cash Reserve (27.5% of budget): $1,925,000

Use this article to help educate your constituency. Knowing the direction you need to take will enable you to plan proactively. Over time, the results will include greater effectiveness in your position, an enhanced position for your school vis-à-vis risk management, and ultimately a superior place for children to learn.

Selling PPRRSM to the Board

ISM has listed five consequences of failing to fund both Physical Plant Replacement, Repairs, and Special Maintenance (PPRRSM) and deferred maintenance, including:
- hazardous conditions inside and outside of the buildings;
- spaces becoming unusable;
- unattractive interiors and exteriors of buildings and grounds;
- missed enrollment due to not meeting prospective parents' expectations of an independent school environment; and
- poor fiscal management due to plant system inefficiencies.

Given that this budget line will constitute 5% to 7% of the school's annual operations budget, it is imperative that the Board of Trustees understands and supports a position that will fund this program (both PPRRSM and deferred maintenance). Ideally, this will be addressed in the Board's quadrennial strategic planning process. However, what can you, as the Business Manager and/or Facilities Manager, do to "get the Board's attention"?

- **Ensure that your Building and Grounds (B&G) Committee (or equivalent) is well informed** through your facilities audit, safety walkarounds, analysis of maintenance costs, review of curb appeal, and so on.
- **Get the School Head on board by giving him/her clear examples of what is currently happening and the impact of being proactive.** For example, demonstrate how replacement of windows can reduce heating and maintenance costs, while also improving the learning environment for children. As often as possible, present similar examples to the School Head and the Chair of the Buildings and Grounds Committee, clearly documenting the benefits of the changes. After completing a number of successful projects and demonstrating their value, the School Head and B&G Chair will be able to present compelling information to the Board and become advocates to fully fund PPRRSM.
- **Promote your total campus PPRRSM plan to the administration and staff.** To promote this plan, it will be important to demonstrate through examples how funding this account will benefit everyone. It also shows the faculty and staff that the school is attending to their facilities concerns.
- **When you are given the opportunity to help educate the Board, ensure that you are well prepared to lead a discussion about the PPRRSM program.** Go through the negative aspects, but also stress the positives by explaining how the whole community will benefit from keeping the campus neat, clean, efficient, and in good repair.

When you have the charge to improve your campus, it is unlikely that you will have a blank check. Continue to increase your political capital by considering the following.

- **At first, select projects that will have a high probability of success and impact.** Small, early successes will make it easier to achieve full funding for PPRRSM later.

Some people think the area with the most waste is where they should start, assuming that replacing this system will show the biggest savings. Typically, this is the wrong approach. If there is a lot of waste, then there is a big problem. Big problems take more time, effort, and money to correct—and the results may not return the predicted savings. To assure early success, it may be best to find a smaller project, or even break your large project into smaller segments that can be more easily achieved.

An example might be the replacement of all low-efficiency lighting fixtures on your campus with high-efficiency fixtures. For a campus with a significant square footage that has not already made an effort to replace such lighting, it would be easy to identify hundreds of such fixtures. To replace all of these would be costly and you may not be able to find the needed funding. The best approach would be to select one or two areas on your campus to refurbish, calculate the amount of anticipated savings, and make a recommendation for replacement of these light fixtures. You can monitor the electrical savings over several months to verify the savings. You may then use these savings to promote a campuswide program for replacement of the remaning fixtures. You could use the same process for replacing inefficient windows or HVAC systems. All of these would improve the learning environment and save money. *When trying to make a change, it is important to show early success.*

- **Make the practice of using small successes to sell your program part of your overall facilities management plan.** By making this approach part of your maintenance program, not only will you have numerous examples that can be used to explain the importance for funding, but your staff will feel that they are accomplishing more. *These employees will then naturally promote your plan.*
- **Find as many ways as possible for your maintenance staff to do the work.** Training support staff to perform some of the work that you may be currently contracting can not only save you money, but it will give you better control of the work that is being performed. If you are currently spending thousands of dollars a year upgrading or replacing electrical or plumbing fixtures, it may pay to hire someone with more than a rudimentary knowledge of a trade who could perform the work in house. Depending on the extent of this person's background, he/she may also be able to make recommendations or implement programs that would otherwise have required spending money on a consultant. *This person typically would not have to work full-time on projects that include his/her trade to pay for the salary when the cost is compared to outside contracting.*
- **As the Business Manager or Facilities Manager, take the opportunity to explain the importance of funding PPRRSM to all administrative personnel.** Give examples showing what is in it for them if the facilities that directly support them are upgraded when needed. If they see how this can improve their world, they will be only too happy to help promote your position. *You do not want to set the wrong expectations for anyone, so be realistic and mention the need to prioritize what will be done and when.*
- **Get everyone involved.** Be sure to identify all stakeholders who will be affected and how each would benefit from a fully funded PPRRSM program. Remember that this list will include every constituent in the school community. When you do upgrade or replace systems in the school, be sure

to let everyone know you have done so. Too often, school administrators do not promote the work that is done behind the scenes, even though it makes a huge difference to the quality of the educational experience for students and staff members. Although you may only report a few of the projects within the program, if successfully implemented, these projects will help to perpetuate the funding needed to assure that you are providing the best facilities possible. *What will sell your plan more than all the Board members talking to happy parents, students, and staff?*

Trustees want to do everything they can to improve the quality of the learning environment. You must demonstrate how funding PPRRSM is one of the best ways to assure that quality remains high so the school can promote itself as an institution that parents are proud to have their children attend.

Limited-Area, Moderate-Cost Space Reconfigurations

Many private-independent schools, especially those without high schools, find themselves on small parcels of land with little hope of purchasing contiguous acreage. Their leaders, searching for additional classroom space and buildings, are often staggered by the costs of buying land for a completely new (or second) campus. They are financially and emotionally defeated by the apparent alternative: relocating the school for a year or more, razing the buildings, and then returning to a campus that is fresh, exciting, and more functional.

Creative approaches to your current space can, however, transform your campus into a jewel barely recognizable as its former self—in a relatively short time and for moderate capital costs. In preparation for your next strategic or long range planning event, you, as Board President, may wish to include on your annual Board agenda an explicit charge to investigate space reconfiguration scenarios capable of (1) adding significantly to total space-under-roof; (2) providing more flexibility for office space and for medium- and large-group class sessions and other kinds of assemblies; (3) upgrading electrical, roofing, and other infrastructure components; and (4) upgrading the school's curb appeal from all angles.

As you derive your upcoming year's committee structure from your annual Board agenda, include the following items in the written charge(s) for one or more of your committees (including the Head Support and Evaluation Committee).

- Ask your School Head, with the Management Team, to:
  - develop an initial list of pedagogical, curricular, cocurricular, faculty development, and other functions that can be enhanced, and for which physical upgrades can contribute to such enhancements;
  - create a facilities chart indicating the locations of all non-load-bearing walls—expect to contract with an outside professional to confirm data of this sort;
  - survey the faculty's storage needs beyond current capacity, and develop an aggregate new-storage square-footage estimate; and
  - develop a description of the ideal electronic configurations (infrastructure) needed to enhance curricular and cocurricular effectiveness.

- With these ministudies in hand, develop at least two (competing) space-reconfiguration scenarios in which, in at least one scenario,
  - non-load-bearing walls are moved from their current positions or removed altogether;
  - a second floor is constructed, using its own load-bearing systems to "straddle" the current first floor (or, if the current first floor can support a second, without the special expense and special design components otherwise implied);
  - covered courtyards are created from what is now open space, turning minimally used areas into assembly areas, dining areas, all-weather recreation areas, and the like; or
  - "study nooks" are created from ordinary passageways; from the new courtyard(s); or from second-floor media center, assembly, and other areas.

- As the project matures during the year, create exciting case statements (and their accompanying budgets) for the capital campaign that will be developed in support of the campus reconfiguration. Consider engaging an architectural firm to design curb-appeal upgrades that could realistically go hand-in-glove with the new functions and their resulting new structures.

Once the total project costs are estimated, you are ready for your strategic planning or long range planning sessions. Campus reconfiguration will be considered and debated by the whole Board and senior administrators (if "strategic") or by the participants from your constituent groups (if "long range"). Bear in mind that the capital costs of such a high-appeal, limited-cost project can and should be borne by a combination of lead gifts; a well-designed, time-limited campaign; and, if needed, by drawing on some of your cash reserves. Avoid the temptation to incur debt. Projects of this sort have great appeal to your major donors and to all constituents, and should—and can—be funded "up front."

Campus Master Plan Supports Good Decision-Making

No one can really foresee the type or extent of facilities your school will need to serve students effectively over the next 10, 20, 50, or 100 years. Still, decisions have to be made; decisions that will, for better or worse, affect the future—next year or decades down the road.

As School Head, how can you help ensure that current actions will enhance your school's options rather than create roadblocks? That's the role of the campus master plan.

If your school has not developed such a plan, now is the time to get the process under way. You'll add a key strategic planning tool to your arsenal, one that motivates school leaders to examine the institution's situation before the need to grow and change is imminent. As a result, you strengthen the likelihood that your school will be prepared to accommodate future requirements.

The campus master plan provides a foundation for making realistic, well-thought-out projections and decisions. Its goals are to:

- ensure that the school's campus and facilities support its mission, goals, and programs;
- assess existing resources;
- identify facility planning issues;
- establish a process to resolve those issues;
- codify projected needs;
- serve as an instrument for organizing those needs; and
- sharpen the focus on funds and resources required to fulfill projected needs.

The Plan in Action

How does a campus master plan work in the "real life" of a school? Consider the following examples.

The plan can help determine the impact of fundamental decisions—such as the placement of structures, roads, parking lots, and utility service lines—so that you enhance, rather than hinder, future construction and other campus improvements.

You might need to expand the parking area. Should you add onto the existing lot? Make it wider, longer, or both? Or create a new lot on the other side of the building? The master plan notes the potential need to add four classrooms within the next few years. You don't want to install asphalt only to have it torn up to accommodate new construction. As a result of the master plan, you have a much clearer perspective on which of the options makes the most sense.

This document can also identify the need for major decisions concerning the school's future. For example, if the plan confirms that your present campus will not sustain enrollment growth, will you hold student population at its current level or begin plans to identify and develop a new campus?

The campus master plan is a critical component in long-range capital improvements. As you determine the need for additional buildings, athletic fields, property, etc., you must also identify sources of funds to support these projects. A well-developed plan helps ensure that goal-setting and financial considerations remain closely linked.

This plan can also have an impact on the school's image and appearance, encouraging coordinated design and enhancement of the overall campus atmosphere as changes are made to structures and grounds.

The Components of a Master Plan

Your school's current situation and the goals defined by the strategic and/or long range plans are the key components in creating a campus master plan. Your approach might be simply to ask and answer a series of basic questions, or you might need to engage in a much more complex process designed, for example, to support a major capital fund drive.

Generally, it is worth the money to engage a professional, such as a member of an architectural firm, to assist with plan development. Access to this level of expertise and advice can help you consider all the angles, provide you with current projections for land use in your area, and determine whether or not your current site can support the projects you have planned.

If you cannot afford an architect, assemble a team comprised of members of your school community who have expertise in construction, real estate, the legal profession, etc. While not ideal, this approach allows your school to develop a basic plan, one that will serve while you gather sufficient funds to create a more formal and extensive document.

The elements of a good campus master plan include:

- identification of improvements that are needed to allow the school to fulfill its mission;
- definition of the specific physical characteristics of the campus you want, including the enrollment you project in your strategic or long range plan;
- a fresh look at the land and buildings you have, reassessing the best use of each;
- a list of campus activities that currently conflict with each other. This might indicate a need for additional space to support these programs;*
- identification of sensitive issues that need to be considered, such as the preservation of historic campus features, open spaces, and environmentally sensitive areas;
- major components of the school program that impact the use of land, such as curriculum, athletics, parking, and general campus circulation patterns for pedestrians;
- marketing strategies that have an effect on facilities and land use. (For example, you might decide you want to attract students from a new geographic area. One strategy is to provide transportation via school-owned vehicles. Where will you park the buses?);
- proper placement and capacity of utility services to maximize their effectiveness for the school while minimizing the cost to provide such services;
- accessibility of your campus by persons with disabilities;
- accessibility of your campus by the general public;
- fire and other life safety issues;

17

- campus security;
- transportation management (i.e., determining vehicle routes, storage of buses and vans, etc.);
- energy conservation; and
- development of properties beyond your campus borders.

Your campus master plan, whether professional or homegrown, is a tool for keeping your school on track. As such, it should undergo a full review in conjunction with any major planning effort and should be updated as needed.

Put Your Planning Team to Work

Whether an architect or an in-house team is spearheading the project, involve representatives of your constituencies in the process of drafting the plan. You'll want to tap one or more members from each of these groups: Board, faculty, staff, students (if age appropriate), parents, alumni, prominent donors, and key members of your extended community, such as a zoning board official.

You might also include an influential neighbor to facilitate your ability to address issues that affect the properties and people in close proximity to your school.

This involvement creates ownership in the plan and ensures a variety of perspectives. The scope of the plan, the goals set by the school's planning documents, and the expertise required will determine whom you ask to be part of the process, how you group those participants to address aspects of the plan, and what level of time commitment will be required to do the job.

Once the plan has been drafted, share the results with your school community. Emphasize that the plan is simply that—a plan, not a promise for the future. Stress that refinements will be necessary as your school matures.

You might create a special "campus master plan report" or cover the highlights in the school newsletter. In addition, hold at least one meeting for the entire school community on this topic.

A separate session might be advisable when the plan is first introduced or when major revisions are made. However, updates can be incorporated into one of the school's regular annual meetings. In all instances, provide an opportunity for constituents to ask questions and comment on your work.

In the meeting, be sure to:
- describe how the planning process was carried out and who participated;
- review the projected capital improvements;
- summarize the existing conditions and their impact on the projected improvements; and
- describe your next steps in the planning process.

Such meetings give you an opportunity to share your vision for the school. If you are planning capital improvements, you can also "prime the pump" with potential future donors.

At the conclusion of these meetings, evaluate the reactions and comments of the community. Their feedback may result in modifications to the plan.

As components of the plan are modified or achieved, keep the lines of communication open via your newsletter. That way those who participated in the process and the entire school community stay informed.

Once the process of creating your plan is complete, you will have added a key document to use in setting your school's course for the future. When you encounter a school campus that is attractive and that fully supports the mission of the school, it's no accident—it's the result of a thorough, well-developed campus master plan.

---

* Note that space problems do not necessarily indicate a need for additional construction. These issues can often be addressed through scheduling strategies and/or a space usage assessment.

A Maintenance Plan Extends the Useful Life of Facilities

It is incumbent on Board Chairs and Heads to ensure that maintenance of current facilities is not overlooked or shortchanged. Major components of your facilities need to be maintained appropriately and consistently so they do not impede or otherwise detract from the programmatic excellence you seek to sustain.

A deferred maintenance/replacement plan identifies those existing building and campus components that require both regular annual attention and replacement (and thus significant dollars) at some time in the future. This type of maintenance has little donor appeal and should be provided for via the budgeting process.

Examples of such building components include roofs, masonry upkeep, windows, doors, water heater and tank, boilers, air-conditioning systems, parking lots and driveways, sidewalks, and playing fields. For example, you'll find it difficult to secure donor funding for a new roof on the middle school building. New playing fields have donor appeal; reseeding a tired playing field does not.

A maintenance plan need not be complicated. Do an inventory of your existing building components listing each one. Note how often it needs to receive maintenance, the projected cost of the maintenance, the estimated useful life, and the projected date and cost of replacement. If your school does not have experienced personnel on its staff, a Board member, parent, or alumnus with the appropriate training may be willing to offer the time and talent to this process.

If your building components have warranties, those documents will be good resources on preventive maintenance needs (a roof is a good example)—what needs to be done, how often, and by whom. Some warranties require the owner regularly to maintain the component, so it is doubly important not to void the warranty by failing to take appropriate maintenance steps.

Stage the plan over several years to allow the school to incorporate the necessary funds in its budget. (See the accompanying chart, "Sample Maintenance Plan," on the next page for a simple example.)

Schools will find it easy to gather the information but much harder to commit funding in the budget. Your preventive maintenance plan will succeed if you set up a facilities replacement savings account.

The Finance Committee should commit to budgeting a percentage of the replacement value of your facilities each year to provide necessary dollars to ensure that the plan is more than just a piece of paper. Many schools strive for a fund that represents 2.5% to 3.0% of the replacement value of the facilities.

This savings account, known as a PPRRSM fund (Provision for Plant Renewal, Replacement, and Special Maintenance), should be an annual charge to your operating budget, with the funds moving into a separate account to fund current and future repairs, replacements, and special maintenance. The funds accumulated in your PPRRSM account can be counted as part of the cash reserve.

As dollars are spent, the next budget process replenishes the fund. If you are just getting started and this goal is too ambitious, then commit to setting aside a minimum of 1% of the replacement value annually and work toward increasing the percentage in subsequent years. Schools with greater financial resources and/or facilities that are more complex may want to have an independent building engineer survey their facilities to create a maintenance plan.

As new or extensively renovated buildings are added to the campus, your school should adjust its preventive maintenance plans to incorporate these facilities immediately. Even though new, they need the same care and attention to extend their useful life as buildings that have served your school for 40 years.

With appropriate attention to your maintenance plan and the discipline to set aside funds for large maintenance projects, your school will be well on its way to extending the useful life of its facilities and, by inference, strengthening the programs and services that are integral to the mission of your school.

Sample Maintenance Plan

Sources of funds	Year Component Put in Service	Est. Useful Life	2003	2004	2005	2006	2007	2008
Carry over from previous year (if unspent)			0	12,000	33,800	15,422	54,279	24,496
Preventive maintenance budget			35,000	36,050	37,132	38,245	39,393	40,575
Restricted endowment—facilities maintenance			10,000	10,200	10,404	10,612	10,824	11,041
Allocation from accumulated PPRRSM funds			15,000	15,000	15,000	15,000	15,000	15,000
Total			**60,000**	**73,250**	**96,336**	**79,279**	**119,496**	**91,112**
Upgrade electrical system in field house	1977	30					35,000	
Replace roof on middle school	1985	20			50,000			
Replace air handling unit in lower school	1988	15		9,000				
Replace walk-in freezer in kitchen	1987	16	15,000					
Resurface upper school parking lot	1998	5	18,000					
Recover seats in theater	1975	30				10,000		
Replace heating system in upper school	1948	60						45,000
Replace heating system in lower school	1947	60					45,000	
Tuck point stone walls	Various	50		15,000	15,000	15,000	15,000	15,000
Replace existing gutters with copper	Various	40	15,000	15,450	15,914			
Total			**48,000**	**39,450**	**80,914**	**25,000**	**95,000**	**60,000**
Surplus/Deficit			**12,000**	**33,800**	**15,422**	**54,279**	**24,496**	**31,112**

The Role of the Board's Buildings and Grounds Committee

Rather like the Finance Committee, it is hard to imagine a school that would not have a Buildings and Grounds Committee. Its role is complementary to the Finance Committee, caring for the current facility (including grounds) and planning for the facility's development, reinvention, and sometimes expansion into the future. ISM's metric provides the role of the Buildings and Grounds Committee. This article will fully articulate what that metric includes.

Membership of the Committee should not be limited to Trustees, and the actual composition depends on the needs of the strategic plan/strategic financial plan as laid out in the Board's annual agenda and the Buildings and Grounds Committee charge. The following guidelines are suggested.

1. The Chair should be a Trustee.
2. The Vice-Chair should be a Trustee in training for the Chair's position.
3. One member should also be a member of the Finance Committee to coordinate the strategic financial plan and annual budgeting process.
4. The Business Manager and Facilities Manager are voting members.
5. There should be at least two non-Trustees.
6. The size of the committee (at least six members) should reflect the work it must do.

Create a rubric for annual evaluation of the Buildings and Grounds Committee's work (see the accompanying rubric), and to ensure that no element is forgotten.

The score can be used to:
– inform the metrics,
– provide guidance around priorities,
– compare progress from year to year, and

Buildings and Grounds Evaluation Rubric

Element	Definition	Max Score	Actual Score
Facilities Audit	There is a facilities audit and it is updated annually.	10	
	We communicate PPRRSM needs on a five-year rolling basis to the Finance Committee.	10	
	Each year's facility needs are met.	20	
Master Campus Development Plan	There is a Master Campus Development Plan and it is up-to-date.	5	
	The Master Campus Development Plan is in use.	5	
Land Acquisition Plan	There is a Land Acquisition Plan and it is up-to-date.	5	
	The Land Acquisition Plan is in use.	5	
Safety	The Buildings and Grounds Committee has a school safety walk checklist.	10	
	The Buildings and Grounds Committee does a safety walk around the school once a month.	10	
	Action items are remedied in a timely way.	20	
Insurance	Appropriate property insurance is in place and monitored annually.	10	
Risk Management	There is a Business Continuation Plan and the Committee monitors it annually.	10	
	Insurance is in place to pay for facilities to keep the school operating in the event of damage.	5	
	Grand Total	125	

– give more energy than a yes/no might provide.

All items must be attended to and any deficits built into both the quadrennial strategic planning process and/or into the annual administrative agenda. Note that this committee includes both strategic and operational components. It is important for the committee to understand that it functions as a Board committee and must look to the Board for its charge to operate and makes recommendations to the Board for action. It also functions as a school support committee and thus makes recommendations to the School Head for action. It has no power to act unilaterally outside these constraints.

With regard to safety, the Buildings and Grounds Committee must understand that this is foremost on the minds of parents. While it is not the committee members' responsibility to consider emotional and social safety, physical safety from a facilities point of view is a crucial aspect of the committee's task. Consider the following observations from tours ISM Consultants have undertaken.

- Doors to the roof not locked.
- No ability to access eye-wash stations in science laboratories due to obstructions.
- No crash bar on doors leading to the outside.
- Chemicals in cabinets that were not locked in rooms with no supervision.

The Buildings and Grounds Committee's ability to "see" these kinds of things and remedy them is crucial to the risk management process. While other elements of its charge are strategic and can be done over a period of months or even years, the safety walk-around is a monthly activity that needs vigilance and constant attention.

The Buildings and Grounds Committee also has a vital role to play when it comes to implementing the purchase of property and/or the development of new/renovated facilities. In these circumstances, it may wish to expand the membership of the committee for the duration of that work and ensure it has appropriate expertise to advise the Board.

The Buildings and Grounds Committee's job has several facets, ranging from planning that impacts the strategic plan/strategic financial plan (campus master development plan and land acquisition plan), to annual planning impacting next year's budgeting (facilities audit), to safety and risk management (business continuation, insurance, and safety processes). Working as a volunteer/professional partnership ensures that the school has mission appropriate facilities that will meet the needs of this and the next generation of students, a key element in supporting the Board's viability objective.

Keep Evolving Program Needs on Your Facilities 'Radar'

Keeping mission squarely in mind, what programs and services will private-independent schools need to offer in the next 10 years to remain competitive? How do they influence the planning and design of new—or adaptation of existing—school buildings? As Board President, remind your committees to consider facility essentials 7–10 years ahead of need.

ISM encourages schools to have a long-range property/facilities plan in place and in use. With this in mind, it is prudent for Boards and School Heads to keep their eyes on the horizon when planning for an upgrade/adaptation of an existing facility or designing one from scratch.

While it is difficult to plan using a "crystal ball" outlook, there are trends that you need to consider. If your planning document calls for significant shifts in program, changes in facilities and services may include:

- computer use (e.g., laptops, personal digital assistants, and wireless networks) that can take place anywhere;
- wider Internet access—triple what you think is enough;
- expanded use of technology as younger teachers with greater computer literacy than the previous generation of teachers come into classrooms. Students, as well, will come to school as early as kindergarten with basic computer skills under their belt;
- more "hands-on," high-tech multimedia production facilities as the definition of visual and performing arts is expanded to make use of the tools of the 21st century;
- classrooms without walls—interactive learning that can take place anywhere and at any time. Imagine a traveling science lab that introduces seventh-graders to complex life at a nearby pond;
- team teaching and nonchronological age groupings of students;
- expanded interdisciplinary curricula;
- distance learning studios to bring specialized teachers to your students (as well as allowing you to serve home-schooled students for a fee);
- use of these same electronic studios to produce parent and community-based learning programs geared to support parents with child rearing;
- a library and media center that offers more technology and fewer shelves for books;
- athletic facilities to serve an ever-expanding array of sports and other activities, not only for your school community but as a resource (via rental) to your locality;
- the need for increased perimeter and interior security on campus to respond to increasing safety concerns;
- support buildings to maintain and house your expanded fleet of buses and other vehicles, as government mandates greater use of common transportation in an effort to conserve diminishing nonrenewable energy;
- support services and programs, shared with schools, colleges and universities, religious institutions, museums, social service agencies, etc. For example, visualize your school as the neighborhood copy center, or the accounting and purchasing department for a number of organizations (all for a fee, of course). In partnership with your school, these agencies, in turn, could offer your students real-life experiences to facilitate their community service or work-study experience; and
- expanded food-services facilities that are equipped to offer a variety of meal options—not only for your students, but on a fee basis for dual-working parents and senior citizens.

As you build and renovate, strive to make space as flexible as possible. More often than not, you will be using the space differently five years from now. Each school will decide its own course; yours needs to be incorporated into a strategic plan. Because most of these ideas require funds, start now to identify and cultivate donors who can help your school fulfill its dreams (and mission). Don't overlook the need to adjust your operating budget to shift or add funds for new initiatives when developing your strategic plan.

Keep these ideas on your "radar" as you think and plan for facilities that will place your school in the forefront—making you more attractive to the next generation of mission-appropriate students. Strategic planning calls for creative thinking, but allows for some "what ifs" as well. What should your school look like in the next 10, 20, or more years?

Land: Always Your School's Best Investment

If your school has a quality program, expect it to thrive and grow—and, as it grows, to need more land.

In ISM's work with thousands of schools, we have not found a single one that complained about owning too much property. However, any number of schools deeply regret not acquiring land when they had the opportunity.

Consider how many schools in recent years started as small, neighborhood elementary programs and became K–12 schools with the need for additional classrooms, buildings, parking spaces, and playing fields. Consider the number that have grown from 150 to 750 students. Consider the benefits of being able to build faculty housing and rent it at reasonable rates if your community becomes excessively high-priced and quality living is out of reach. Consider the increase in land values around your school over the past 30 years; the real-dollar growth no doubt has been significant.

A Board of Trustees must look 100 years into the future, ensuring that the school can fulfill its mission and meet its goals without having land values limit program or planning decisions for future Boards.

Example: A Need for More Land

I&P Academy (our fictional PK–12, coed day school) has learned the tough lesson of having nowhere to grow. Over a period of years, classrooms in this school have become filled to capacity, and each fall there have been extensive waiting lists in the lower grades.

Demographics indicate that the trend will continue. The Board sees the potential for adding at least four classrooms, but the current site cannot accommodate additional construction.

Ten years earlier, property adjoining the campus had been offered for sale at an affordable price. Today this land is covered with expensive homes.

I&P Academy has three options—ignore the opportunity to expand; attempt to sell the current property and relocate to a new, larger site, with all the accompanying expense, disruption, and potential loss of enrollment; or set up a satellite campus, which creates its own set of management challenges.

In addition, I&P Academy did not anticipate the dramatic growth in girls' athletics over the past 30 years. Like many other schools, I&P wants to continually upgrade its offerings, but does not have adequate space to develop both soccer and lacrosse programs for girls.

Lacrosse is an excellent example of changes that can impact space needs. It was found only in the Northeast and mid-Atlantic states two decades ago. But this fast-moving, exciting team sport has spread rapidly, with private school leagues forming throughout the country. However, it takes space—the playing field is similar in size to football's or soccer's.

Can your school's current site support not only additional athletics, but also educational and/or technological advances that may challenge your school's land capacity in the 21st century?

How Much Is Enough?

Regardless of your school's character, size, or type, 40 acres is the bare minimum amount of land needed if you have, or potentially will have, secondary grades. Sixty acres should be your "necessary" figure, and 100 acres the ideal.

Of course, schools can exist with less property, but they contend with having too little space to construct parking lots, new academic buildings, athletic fields, and outdoor study areas. Public school norms for acreage do not apply because a private school campus houses unique operations such as admission, development, business management, transportation, maintenance, public relations, alumni relations, and active parent programs and fund-raising events. In fact, a private school's needs relate more closely to a college than to a public school.

In addition, private schools encourage or even require participation in athletics and activities, and many have a "no-cut" policy for sports teams and performance groups. It is not unusual to have 70% to 90% of the student body involved in one or the other at any given time. All this requires space.

Other Benefits of Additional Land

Historically, land has been one of the best investments for individuals. It can be even more attractive for a nonprofit school because property that is adjacent to the existing campus, or noncontiguous parcels that are being used for educational purposes such as a ropes course or pond ecology, may be exempt from taxation, depending upon the laws of the state and locality in which the real estate is located.

In fact, property can constitute a pseudo-endowment. Acquiring parcels of land can later bring tremendous financial benefit through sale or lease. One school, for example, purchased a large dairy farm located near an expressway exit beyond a city's urban sprawl. The campus was built well back from the intersection.

Thirty years later, the sprawl reached the school, and the land became very valuable. Property along the exit road was leased to an upscale shopping center, producing a substantial annual income.

Other portions of the farm were sold to developers, who constructed expensive homes. The school kept a buffer of land to meet future needs and retain the esthetic qualities of its open, pastoral setting. The land sales paid for the original purchase, several buildings and athletic fields, and established a sizeable endowment.

Another school began buying up nearby houses, which it rented to faculty, enabling it to attract and keep high-quality, "breadwinner" teachers. Yet another swapped land it owned on the outskirts of town for a downtown office building and parking garage. The subsequent leasing and parking revenues, along with other swaps and utilization of its real-estate assets, have built one of the largest per-student endowments in the nation.

Seize the Opportunity

Hold onto property your school already owns, and take every opportunity to purchase land that is contiguous to or near your site when it becomes available. Pass up the chance and you risk the fate of a private-independent secondary school that initially bought what it thought was enough land for current and future needs. The property was inexpensive and was located in the middle of nowhere.

A parcel next to the school's entrance later became available, but the Board passed up the opportunity to buy it. When the school later found itself in dire need of additional land for playing fields, it was surrounded by high-priced residences, polo fields, country clubs—and the elementary division of a competing private school, located on that parcel near the entrance.

It's very common for property adjacent to a school's existing campus to carry an inflated price tag because the owners think the school has "deep pockets" and will be anxious to buy. They're right! Although you may not want to pay the price, you should not sit by and let someone else snap up the land. Consult with an attorney experienced in this area of the law. There may be ethical and legal ways to acquire the property at close to fair market value.

A word of caution: Land should be purchased with money raised beforehand; avoid borrowing funds. Mortgages can become chronic problems, "robbing" money each month that should go to programs and enhancements. And there's always the risk that, once the mortgage is acquired, Board members will consider the current problem solved, halt fund raising for the property, and pass the debt responsibility on to their successors.

Retiring the debt then becomes a major challenge. No one wants to make a financial contribution for something that already exists. It's also difficult to interest prospective donors in paying off the amount; they're much more likely to be interested in buying land for the school.

Unless you already own land that provides ample room for the addition of classrooms, facilities, and fields for the next 100 years, begin scouting the possibilities. Is there adjacent property that is currently available or likely to come on the market? Or do you need to begin searching for land that could become your school's future home?

Create a small Board-level committee—perhaps called the Land Exploration Committee—made up of two Trustees who are savvy about real estate. Charge them with conducting a wide-ranging exploration in your draw area.

Planned Gifts of Property

Cash in hand may not be required to add to your school's land holdings. Property, homes, and other structures can be donated to the school directly or under a form of planned giving known as a life estate.

Either approach benefits both the school and the donor. In the case of a life estate, the contributor receives a tax deduction on the gift. The donor can form a trust with the school that provides income over the donor's lifetime and/or, if a house is involved, allows the donor to live in the dwelling as long as necessary.

In return, the school receives an inheritance that, depending on its type, can be used to expand the campus, sold for needed cash, converted into a faculty home, or rented out for income.

As the phrase implies, planned giving is a long-term approach. Your development personnel must keep their eyes open for such an opportunity, and potential donors must be carefully cultivated over time.

Check with your legal counsel on the procedures and parameters for life estates in your state.

Land Acquisition Plans: Context and Action

How much land is enough? ISM has long recommended that schools acquire a minimum of 40 acres (and ideally 100+ acres). This is particularly true where the school is (or includes) an upper school with its enormous athletic needs. In all our work with schools, ISM has not encountered one that complained of owning too much land, but has found many that regret not acquiring land when they had the opportunity. Today, of course, land is so much more than athletic fields. Schools see the importance of outdoor classrooms, adventure playgrounds, organic gardens, ecological preserves, wetland conservation, and so on.

As a Trustee, ensure that your school can fulfill its mission and meet its goals without having land values and space limitations hamper program or planning decisions for future Boards and Management Teams. Many schools older than 100 years have wonderful grounds and buildings but are surrounded by urban development. When visionary founders, school leaders, and Boards originally bought the land, there were only open fields. Schools are often landlocked in urban and suburban settings, with no obvious chance of expansion. What should you do?

When thinking of the Board's mission statement—ensuring the viability of the school to the next generation of students—creating and renewing your land acquisition plan is of strategic importance. This is one of the three documents every school should have for the school's buildings and property, including a:

- facilities audit—a 30-year calendar of all the major building/facilities components that will need renewal or replacement such as walls, windows, roofs, air conditioners, heat exchangers, and boilers;
- master campus facilities plan—a 5- to 25-year plan that considers the facilities services the school imagines requiring into the future. The plan also envisions facility placement on the current property footprint to ensure that any building, in the near term, is done in such a way that it supports and does not impede future construction. This is not just related to buildings themselves, but also with the interaction of the inside/outside planning of the entire school property; and
- land acquisition plan—a 50-year ambition with regard to either how to expand the current land footprint (including how the land might be used), or an analysis of school needs that might lead to relocation to a space with more land flexibility.

Creating the Documents

These three documents lead from one to another. Knowing what you have, and defining the issues associated with that, enables each document to support and amplify the other two. We recommend the following procedure.

- The Buildings and Grounds Committee members—including the Business Manager and Facilities Manager—work together to create the facilities audit. If you do not have one, this typically takes about a year. There is little cost, since the work and analysis can be done by your committee experts and your contractors. With this in place, you have an excellent data set to know assets and liabilities of your current property.
- The Buildings and Grounds Committee can then move to the master campus facilities plan. Understand that, in the 20th century, this typically meant the buildings on the property only. Little attention was paid to the property as a whole, except to be assured that there was enough space for parking and entrance/egress in a safe manner. In the 21st century, schools are required to consider water management, waste management, and school grounds for outdoor learning. The master campus facilities plan should include:
  – future building needs,
  – future play space needs,
  – future environmental uses of the property,
  – potential relocation of current functions,
  – implications of technology use, and
  – implications of environmental standards.
- This then leads to the property acquisition plan. Just as the master campus facilities plan has strategic plan/strategic financial plan implications, so the property acquisition plan is clearly a strategic document.
  a. Begin by assessing the property you currently have. Does your school own or has it acquired the rights to at least 40 contiguous acres if you have a suburban or rural campus, or one city block if you are in an urban location? These are viability standards that allow the school to deliver a premier program that can adjust to changing client interests and competitive circumstances.
  b. Is the property you currently own below the viability standard noted above? If so, incorporate into your strategic plan the resources needed to acquire adjacent properties as they become available.
  c. If you are totally landlocked, begin discussions on whether you might move your school to a new location. Without strategic planning and action now, affordable land or property in another area may not be available in five or 10 years.
  d. What restrictions, if any, do you have on your current property? Have municipal authorities placed enrollment caps, building density limitations, etc., on your existing properties? Can those restrictions be removed or altered? If not, these conditions may contribute to a decision to move the school to another location, while land is still available.
  e. If your school is landlocked, what needs might property acquisition alleviate? In expensive locations, housing for faculty and administrators is a true concern, given the incomes needed for home purchase or the travel distance from affordable accommodations.
  f. Charge a member of the Buildings and Grounds Committee with the monitoring function (e.g., the systematic tracking of tendencies or anticipated directions in demographic development, zoning changes, land and housing prices). Maintain a database to help "catalog" the urgency (or not), as assigned by the B&G Committee, of potential land acquisition.

g. Assign a member of the committee to explore systematically and proactively land purchase opportunities, in areas implied by the assessment and monitoring process.

If you determine the school does not need to acquire land at this time, reviewing land needs and availability should be a part of each strategic planning process. Boards should always be aware of the possibilities of purchasing property for their schools—and be prepared to act quickly when the opportunity arises.

Actual Purchase

If you determine you need to acquire land or adjacent buildings, ensure the property does not come with "hidden issues." Be sure to engage your school's legal counsel to guide you through the various challenges. The following checklist provides some considerations before purchasing any property.

1. Physical characteristics of the property
2. Existing conditions on the property
3. Environmental impact study
4. Title issues
5. Infrastructure to serve the property
6. Comprehensive plan policies, zoning laws, and Shoreline Management Act policies and regulations (for properties within shoreline areas)
7. Critical area regulations
8. Discretionary decisions by city or county councils
9. Approvals and permits required
10. Impact fees
11. Procedural steps and time frames
12. Community relations

Sources of funding include a campaign, a quiet major gifts ask, the use of cash reserves, or a combination of sources. Be cautious in your investigations. Your neighbors may not appreciate your long-term plans and/or they may see you as an easy way to make money, thinking you have deep pockets. Keep in mind that you may not have an immediate need for the property. Also, avoid the temptation to become a landlord, if that might take your eye off your real mission.

This ongoing process integrates care for your current property, deep understanding of future needs, and vision for the future. Planning for land acquisition is worthy of the Board's time as it maintains viability to the next generation.

Facilities: When You Run Out of Money

Consider this case study drawn from a real example in 2012.

A school has positive enrollment and is committed to expanding facilities that reflect the school's commitment to project-based learning, inquiry, and differentiation. The school is committed to diversity reflected in an admission policy inviting application from a wide range of students with a mix of educational needs. Class sizes are between 20 and 30. The faculty is excellent and has been involved in the facilities planning process from the start. The Board is enthusiastic about the new construction project, as is the parent body. The capital campaign kicks off with apparent success.

Before all the money is in the bank, the school begins the building process. Unfortunately, the campaign is not as successful as was anticipated. The Building and Grounds Committee meets with the architects and builder, and they slash classroom size and "unnecessary" rooms not deemed critical to the main function of the building.

Returning from summer break, teachers discover that their plans are unfulfilled; the program they had envisioned is now a challenge to implement. Some find that their classrooms are 200 square feet smaller than they had anticipated.

The issues this case study brings up are instructive for Boards and School Heads as they plan capital campaigns. This is not an uncommon situation—when we ask Facilities Managers why things are the way they are, we are often met with rolled eyes and the phrase "financial realities."

What counsel can be offered? ISM notes the following facts.

- Trustees (who pass through in their rotating terms of service) and School Heads (who typically stay less than 10 years at any given school) do not serve through the lifespan of one student in a K–12 school. In other words, the actions you take carry limited accountability. The facilities you build—and the teachers who teach in them—have to live with your decisions for decades and generations after you have moved on.
- In contemporary teaching environments, well-planned facilities—providing flexibility in space for variable student groupings and an ability to implement various teaching pedagogies—must not be compromised. For example, in the case study above, reducing a classroom size from 950 square feet to 700 square feet with a class load of 25 will not eliminate the ability to teach. It does, however, make it difficult (if not impossible) to group students variably (rather than have them sit in the same place all day) and to use certain pedagogies that require group work and collaboration (rather than lecture). Form must follow function. Where function follows form, the impact of design changes can hinder the delivery of the school's mission. Teachers can overcome many obstacles, but there is always a point at which they cannot overcome the physical limitations of their environment.
- Environment matters. ISM does not "advocate" one pedagogy over another, or one teaching style over another. We do advocate, strongly, that the mission implications of architecture—the intersection of time, space, program, and people—must be worked out by each school such that the mission can be delivered with integrity.

We therefore recommend that:

- strategic planning and strategic financial planning be at the foundation of any capital planning exercise;
- facilities planning includes the faculty as an essential part of the design process to create mission-appropriate, student-centered buildings;
- capital campaigns are preceded by feasibility studies to ensure that the aims of the campaign can be realized, and so the Case for Support engages the school's donors to invest generously;
- new construction should not commence until the goals of the campaign are assured; and
- reductions in funding that result in downsizing of the project do not become a decision process that leaves faculty out in the cold. Changes in scope should be identified and determined by the same interest groups that approved the original design.

While realities in capital campaigns can force a school to rethink its original objectives, decisions made in haste and in isolation result in much more profound consequences than might be apparent to a Trustee or committee member. In attempting to carry out their duty in one direction (fiscal responsibility), they may lose sight of their duty in the other direction (mission delivery). The inclusion of the faculty in such decisions is crucial at the beginning of these campaigns—and that inclusion must continue to the end of the project, particularly when changes in scope are under discussion. Doing this will ensure that, despite unforeseen fiscal realities, teaching requirements will be fulfilled.

The Eight Steps of Facility Planning

As your school plans to renovate current facilities or build new ones, it is critical to know ahead of time the steps necessary to determine their final cost. This process takes time, but the time invested in the earliest stages of facility planning yields two benefits. You realize major savings by defining your needs and avoiding mistakes. You also avoid the embarrassment of setting a premature fund-raising goal that fails to support the fully realized project.

The following eight-stage process assures that the school will have a facility that meets the needs of the program and falls within the school's funding capabilities. The "value engineering" (the changes ordered when a building costs $4 million but the school can only afford $3 million) is built into—rather than results from—the process.

Step 1: Quantitative Review

This overview specifies the number and types of spaces required and provides rough square-footage for each space. The estimates are determined by:
- the people who will occupy the space, based on the space they currently occupy or have seen in other schools; or
- architects, who typically use guidelines published by the state education department, faculty planning groups, and/or the firm's experience.

If guidelines are used to estimate areas, they may be too liberal or conservative. Guidelines tend to reflect a standard space, not the space required by the mission and teaching methodologies of your school.

The totals of the area of individual spaces result in the estimated net square footage of the buildings. This total does not include hallways, stairs, mechanical and boiler rooms, restrooms, or even the thicknesses of walls.

To estimate the total gross area (and the cost) for all construction, multiply the net area (n) by a factor of 1.4. This factor is derived from an average as reported by schools in the construction process. The total area required should not be reduced without an architect's guidance. While Step 1 can be completed without hiring an architect, his or her professional opinion can be invaluable as you face these initial decisions.

Step 2: Qualitative Overview

The key activity in the qualitative overview is the writing of your educational specifications that are unique to your school and its program. The specifications include careful descriptions of the activities to be performed in each space, the size of the groups to be included, services needed, and relationships to other spaces. This process provides a more refined estimate of the net area.

In addition, computer-aided design (CAD) programs have given rise to a new development in educational specification writing and involve the architectural firm earlier in the planning. If the floor area of furniture and equipment (F&E) is specified, the maximum amount of F&E anticipated in each space can be placed in various configurations on computer-generated diagrams, with appropriate spacing for maneuvering of people, carts, and materials. This simulation test of each room's area gives feedback to the future user of the space.

As your administrative team develops the qualitative educational specification, it is possible to achieve detailed control over the size necessary for each space based on the activities, group sizes, and facilitating F&E. You, not the architect, make the decision to have, for example, three, not five, computers in a classroom and to delete a side counter while maintaining a large sink.

Such planning is not possible unless all F&E occupying floor space are specified. (Floor space should be occupied only once; e.g., a wastebasket under a table need not be specified, but a waste receptacle under a liquid-soap dispenser in a restroom would be specified.)

Some CAD programs use height dimensions for presenting visual simulations of rooms. If this will be used for some spaces, such as a library or presentation room where lines of vision are critical, then the height dimension can be requested from specification writers.

In ISM's experience, it's not unusual to hear disbelief that furniture is being chosen so soon. Actually, it is not being chosen. Many options (e.g., finish, selection of smaller items) have still been left open, and this may not be in the architect's contract as an appropriate concern. What the users (teachers, administrators, staff) are saying is, "These are the maximum number and/or size of F&E items we want the designer to accommodate." Furniture and equipment selection also aids in remembering activities to specify.

Step 2 results in precise estimates of the net area required by the facility and a comprehensive description of each space. This is planning from the inside out.

Step 3: Cost Estimates

While still rough, cost estimates made at this stage can be informative. Especially important are the estimated costs of furniture and furnishings—they can attract donor interest and may be packaged as a major fund project within a larger campaign.

Draw up your furniture and equipment list and, if applicable, designate catalog numbers and/or vendors. You are not ordering F&E at this point, just generating a fairly precise cost estimate, including inflation based on time of delivery.

Step 4: Schematic Design

Not until this step can the buildings' gross areas be estimated with reasonable accuracy. At this point in the planning process, the architect assumes responsibility for the rest of the project. Floor plans are produced, showing relationships that may have to be revised based on the qualitative educational specifications. Such changes should be agreed upon by the writers of the specifications —not imposed by the architect.

Site planning costs should be very accurate by Step 4's closure.

Step 5: Design Development

The design development stage focuses on the "look" of the structure and campus. Decisions on particular attributes, e.g., fenestration and all dimensions, allow more realistic cost estimation.

Step 6: Construction Documents and Working Drawings

Little input is required from you by the end of this step. Detailed specifications and working drawings are prepared to be studied by those bidding for the construction contract. Another estimate in anticipation of bids is prepared. Alternative bids might be requested to bracket the estimate, allowing for optional projects to be built if bids are low.

Step 7: Bidding

When you accept a bid, you know what the construction will cost, as long as the architect's drawings were accurate and you do not change your mind about the revised educational specifications and selections you have made on items presented by the architect. (Architects may be liable for the cost of their mistakes, thereby not increasing your cost.)

Step 8: Ordering Furniture and Equipment

These costs are associated with F&E orders to outfit your new or renovated facility. Rather than estimate this cost on guidelines of 7% to 15% of construction, why not use the results of Steps 2 and 3 to produce an estimate based on actual lists for each space? When you get the quotes, you know your cost. Add this to Step 7's bid and any allowance for changes or contingencies, you have a firm estimate of costs.

Sequence of Cost and/or Area Estimates of Building Projects
(accuracy increases with each step)

	ES = educational specifications		Type of Area estimate	
Step	Stage of Planning	Basis of Estimate	Net	Gross
1	Quantitative ES overview	Guidelines and past experience	n	1.4n
2	Qualitative ES detailed chapters + CAD	Decide on F&E, drawn on CAD to test space estimates	n (very accurate net, efficient space)	1.4n or less, with architect's permission
3	Cost estimation (architectural programming, the problem statement is complete)	Room-by-room estimates done by architect or program manager, plus Business Manager's estimate of furniture and equipment. Some assumptions regarding building design, timing, and engineering can be placed in computerized programs	same as 2	1.4n, still no design of building, still rough
4	Schematic design (site planning could be done prior to schematic design of interiors)	Relationships and layout drawn	Some compromises possible	Site and building costs more accurate
5	Design development, design drawings	Actual plans	Modules of design with ±10% of ES; modification of size is a consequence of design, not a budgeting move	Highly accurate
6	Construction documents, working drawings	Finishes, hardware, equipment, and all systems	N/a	Architectural specifications are highly detailed, very predictive of cost
7	Bidding, if not collaborative planning	Bid	Proof of the pudding, if no change orders	
8	F&E ordering	Purchase orders, quotes with shipping	Cost is highly accurate	

Facility Design and Strategic Planning

School Heads and Boards of Trustees must pay attention to both the operational and strategic elements of facility planning and design. Facilities might more typically be thought of as operational—while the Board approves the development of new facilities and engages the designer, the school works with the designer to establish needs and solutions. However, both you as School Head and your strategic partner the Board President might take a closer look at this process, which needs more integration than this simple separation of roles assumes.

Consider these "horror" stories.

- A new high school was built in 2007, with the largest capital campaign of the school's history. The design included a language lab and a lecture theater—features more appropriate to the 1950s than to the 21st century.
- An elementary school's design was changed over a summer's construction to meet new budget demands, slashing the size of the second floor classrooms by 30% and eliminating key specialized spaces for learning-needs students.
- A school building, recently erected, had to be demolished to provide parking spaces as required by zoning regulations.
- Because of budget considerations, an academic building was not installed with heating and air-conditioning controls. This now requires the only facilities person to change all controls manually—an operation infrequently carried out because of the time needed, resulting in sometimes unbearably hot and cold temperatures in various classrooms.

It's not hard to find examples similar to these, even if less dramatic. It might be thought that common sense would be an antidote to poor planning and design. But it seems the "excitement" of capital campaigns can bring on their own dynamic, forcing hasty decision-making and ignoring the warning signs of potential issues. The following recommendations are not designed to cover every circumstance, but to suggest broad (yet specific) principles. The School Head and Trustees—with their planning subordinates, the CFO/Facilities Director, Building and Grounds Committee members, and academic leaders—should consider these in their planning and design process.

1. Ensure that strategic planning uncovers issues and seeks information about:
   - the school's enrollment plan with the intent to drive an excess of supply;
   - teachers' and students' program intentions;
   - financial support for facilities and the programs to be delivered in them, i.e., facilities and programs are not separate but integrated areas; and
   - the school's current and potential footprint.
2. Constructing new facilities should not be a cover-up for poor maintenance. Schools often run their facilities into the ground and, when deferred maintenance becomes overwhelming, simply replace the now-inadequate building with another. Instead, through strategic financial planning, ensure that facilities maintenance is funded through the PPRRSM element of the cash reserve. This is a key Finance Committee responsibility for inclusion in strategic planning.
3. Make facilities planning and design integral to strategic planning and strategic financial planning when a capital campaign is envisaged. It is not enough to raise money; it is not enough even to build. School buildings that "look good" are not necessarily buildings that are useful.
4. Include all the people necessary. This is particularly true of academic leaders, faculty, and students. It is not just a pleasantry to include these groups from the beginning to the end of the process but a necessity—and that inclusion is an integral part of the planning, design, and construction process. Strategic planning in and of itself may not include faculty and students; when facilities are on the agenda, they cannot be ignored. They can and should be included in the appropriate Board committees and task forces set up to recommend to the Board before strategic planning. This will undoubtedly include consideration of program (present and anticipated) through strategic academic planning. They can and should be included subsequent to strategic planning as well, right through to the first day of the building's use.
5. Timetables for campaigns can force hasty or poor decision-making. The need to engage donors before their children leave the school often comes up as one rationale for moving quickly. While the practicalities of fundraising cannot be denied, the aphorism "act in haste, repent at leisure" is applicable here. Set the timetable through the strategic planning timeline. While this may mean a lesser engagement by a donor whose child is graduating, it will mean greater engagement by all the donors whose children are still in the school. Key donors appreciate the attention paid to detail and deliberation, and the depth at which the school can answer key questions.

It is not "natural" to associate facilities planning and design with strategic planning, even as campaigns are considered a strategic decision. In an environment where classrooms and libraries are recast as innovation labs, makerspaces, and learning commons, and where we are paying closer attention to the learning environment and its academic impact on students, the School Head and Board President should think more broadly about strategic planning/strategic financial planning to more closely examine the planning and design element of a capital campaign.

Educational Specifications:
The Foundation for the Facility of Your Dreams

Any professional, knowledgeable architect will ask your school for educational specifications—a definition of the "who, what, when, why, and how" for each space in the structure. These "building blocks" make the difference between a generic, restrictive structure and one specifically designed to:

- support your school's mission;
- meet the needs of your program;
- serve the students, faculty, and staff who use the building daily; and
- stay within your budget constraints.

Whether your construction project involves a new building or renovations, educational specifications for each space should address:

- the activities to take place;
- instructional methods and special equipment used both now and in the future;
- the total number and age(s) of students, as well as the number of adults that must be accommodated;
- required services and utilities;
- projected hours of use;
- accessibility concerns (such as delivery of materials); and
- storage needs.

Without these details, your architect may, for example, design the math and science centers' classrooms to facilitate standard lecture-style teaching. That won't suit the process-oriented curriculum you, the School Head, and your staff have planned. You may overlook special needs for lighting, noise control, electricity, security, and other factors.

With these specifications in place, your architect can do a more effective job of designing and costing out your project, and contractors and suppliers can produce bids that are more accurate. You'll also minimize the number of costly change orders and last-minute, decisions that often result from a lack of information.

Developing the Educational Specifications

How can you ensure that all the details are covered? While some schools hire an educational specifications consultant, it is possible to do the job yourself without compromising the quality of the product. Organize an Educational Specifications Team and use the charts that accompany this article.

Establish that the Educational Specifications Team includes:

- the Division Head(s) whose students use the facility;
- one or two teachers representing those who will use the new structure;
- a teacher from another division (to provide perspective);
- the Business Manager;
- the Facilities Manager;
- the representative leading the project. This person can be invaluable to ensure you base expectations on reality and that what you want to build or remodel fits your preliminary budget; and
- the Development Director. In any high-profile project, all must be familiar with the details as you work with potential donors.

The three accompanying charts provide a foundation for mentally "walking through" the details that affect facility design and construction. Add your own items and create more categories, as needed.

Chart A: The Educational Specifications Team uses this chart to determine:

- all activities that could conceivably occur in each specific room or area;
- the number of students and adults each of those areas must accommodate; and
- equipment that has a direct impact on construction.

A thorough consideration of activities, occupancy, and equipment helps you think through the ramifications of that space use. Consider these examples.

- The upper school science lab must accommodate 24 students in four-member teams, needing space for six workstations. This room also needs to incorporate access to natural gas and water, wiring for computers, equipment storage, and provisions for proper disposal of chemicals, among other considerations.
- Besides desks and chairs, a preschool classroom may need to accommodate various activities, all of which may go on at the same time—e.g., manipulatives, artwork, and meal or snack preparation.
- Specialized equipment often needs specialized storage. In the new arts center, the team must decide where to put items when they are not in use. Space may be needed for musical instruments, costumes and sets, easels—even a cherry picker to reach the auditorium lights.

Chart B: The team uses this chart to specify the types and quantities of general furniture and equipment that will be placed in each room or area when construction is completed.

Chart C: This chart concerns 15 key areas. The School Head and Division Head(s) can use this as a guide in writing the program description, a document based on the educational specifications.

Creating the Program Description

Follow these five steps as you develop the program description.

1. **Make a copy of each of the three charts for each room or area in your project**—including the hallways. Even this "simple" space can produce complex questions: How many students must pass through at any one time? Must it accommodate lockers, bulletin boards, or vending machines? Or break-out groups from the adjoining classrooms?
2. **Assign a name or number to each space** that will identify it as the design develops.
3. **In deciding the needs and wishes attached to each space, be as clear and thorough as you can** at this point in the process. Do not place limits on requests. Besides the major elements, you want to identify those important, often

overlooked small-ticket items. While not everything on the "wish list" will be included in the final project, it is easier to delete items now than to add more later. There will be sufficient time during the architect's design development and costing stages to "value engineer" items out of the project, if dreams exceed resources.

4. **Once you complete the forms, tabulate the results.** Refine the wishes and desires, dividing them into two lists: "critical" and "preferable but not essential." Include the latter if funds allow. Describe any considerations that fall outside the standard limits of a construction project (e.g., preserving elements about the "character" of the campus).

5. **Write your project description**—a simple two- to three-page overview that covers the major design considerations and incorporates relevant information about your program, schedule, and campus. Attach the three detailed charts. These four documents become the foundation for the educational specifications for your new facility.

While you want to be detailed and specific in setting educational specifications, avoid tying the architect's hands. Give this professional latitude to design a functional and flexible facility. The goal in creating educational specifications is to provide a clear picture of the "outcome" you expect from your new structure. With this information, the architect can plan, design, and build a facility that reflects the quality of your school and supports its programs.

Chart A: Activities and Equipment (with direct impact on construction)

Project: _____ Name of the Space: _____ Date: _____

ACTIVITIES	STUDENTS/ADULTS	ITEM	QUANTITY
General classroom:		**Wall-mounted equipment:**	
Lecture		Smart boards	
Discussion groups		Bulletin boards	
Small-group work		White boards	
Large-group work		Maps	
Quiet areas		LCD projector	
Computer use		Other (specify)	
Other (specify)		**Communications:**	
Specialized activities:		Telephone	
Arts (specify types)		Intercom	
Science		Other (specify)	
Exercise/athletics			
Meetings		**Specialized equipment/needs:**	
Conference area		Access to water	
In-class restroom		220-volt outlets	
Other (specify)		Natural gas	
Technology:		Refrigeration	
Individual/group workspaces			
Server(s)/access wiring		**Storage:**	
Computer teaching station		Equipment and supplies (specify)	
Computer charging stations		Specialized items (specify)	
Other (specify)			

Chart B: General Furniture and Equipment

Project: _____ Name of the Space: _____ Date: _____

ITEM	QUANTITY	ITEM	QUANTITY
Furniture:		**Audiovisual equipment:**	
Student chairs (types)		Chart stand	
Student desks (type)		Easel(s)	
Teacher chairs		Flip chart	
Teacher desks		Map stand	
Tables (stationary)		Globe	
Tables (folding)		Portable LCD projector	
Bookcases (standard)		Projector screen	
Bookcases (specialized—describe)		Television/DVR	
Shelves (standard)		Camera/video equipment	
Shelves (specialized—describe)		Other (specify)	
Locking file cabinets (2-drawer)			
Locking file cabinets (3-drawer)		**Other equipment:**	
Locking file cabinets (4-drawer)		Photocopier	
Other (specify)		Paper cutter	
Technology:		Laminating machine	
Computers		Other (specify)	
Computer chairs			
Computer tables			
Printers			
Other (specify)			

Chart C: Other Considerations

Project: _____ Name of the Space: _____ Date: _____

Zone:	Public	**Illumination:**	Bright	**Access:**	From inside
	Semi-public		Moderate		From outside
	Restricted		Special		Both
Flexibility:	Expandable		Flexible	**Security:**	Lock
	Versatile		Natural		No lock
	None	**Noise control:**	Required	**Adjacencies:**	Restrooms
Supervision:	Required		None		Library
	Moderate	**Climate control:**	High		Playground
	None		Normal		Other (specify)
View out:	Desirable		Special	**Mechanicals:**	Air-conditioning
	Optional	**Water:**	Tepid		No air-conditioning
	None		Hot	**Special flooring:**	Carpet
View in:	Desirable		Cold		Tile
	Optional	**Electric:**	110v		Both
	None		220v		Other
			Both		

Why Spend Educators' Time Planning Facilities?

Educational specifications are primarily written by teachers, and the process is time-consuming.* To be effective, specifications must encompass research into modern or developing methodologies and, in some cases, reports from site visits to other schools. At the same time, teachers must continue their own teaching and other duties.

The following five questions are commonly asked about the usefulness of educational specifications. The responses reflect the reality of each situation.

1. **We have set school enrollment, division size, and section size. Should we now accept the judgments of a professional—the architect—concerning space requirements? After all, a classroom is a classroom—how can we go wrong by doing what others have done?**

   Reality: During the design process, the architect will meet with teachers, administrators, and staff to gather their perspectives on space and its use in the building. After accruing this information about what teachers are doing now, the architect is ready to design.

   Since architects do not monitor changes in teaching methodologies or learning theory and are not knowledgeable about scheduling options, the building will not reflect educational research or exemplary programs. The building is being designed for past teaching methods and does not anticipate the future.

2. **Our teachers just don't have the time during the day to write educational specifications. Will they be interested if they must work on their own time?**

   Reality: While it is true that teachers are busy with all the duties or tasks required by your school, asking them to assist in the design of the space that they will occupy can be a major component in professional development. Researching new methods being employed in their field, learning how technology can be used in their rooms, and visiting and exchanging ideas with other teachers can be renewing experiences. Teachers seldom experience such renewal, which can reinvigorate enthusiasm for teaching. Don't assume teachers will refuse to complete research on their own time—schools find teachers are often delighted to do so.

3. **Educators cannot accurately forecast the instructional processes and methodologies for the lifetime of a building. Therefore, why ask their opinions?**

   Reality: No one is better prepared to discover what "pioneers" in the field are doing than your bright-light teachers, Curriculum Directors, and Division Directors with curricular and instructional insight. With support and resources, they can become advocates for change. The architect need not be forced to make assumptions regarding education- and mission-related needs. Since assumptions must be made, ask those best prepared to have a vision of the future. Educational practice simply does not change so fast that our best educators are blind to what needs to be done.

4. **It is the architect's responsibility to design a flexible building. If it's flexible, then why describe activities of the near and distant future?**

   Reality: It is impractical to expect complete flexibility; e.g., it is too expensive to expedite conversion of any space to any use. But you could save on construction costs by anticipating which rooms may have specific needs (e.g., natural gas or hot water) in the future. If you can specify multiple uses or conversions of spaces before design, you can achieve good results at lower construction cost.

   Architectural flexibility only contributes to the resulting flexibility of your building; true flexibility in educational space can be achieved or enhanced by precise educational specifications.

5. **If teachers are going to write educational specifications, why do we need an architect?**

   Reality: The educational specifications suggest solutions to the architect and carefully define a space. However, they are not intended to design the room or place the room in a coordinated building design. The teachers provide the design professional with the function of the space, but the architect defines its form.

As you take the time to write educational specifications, be sure that you establish a clear time line with regular progress reports. *Planning takes time*, especially if growth of understanding is to occur. Discuss programmatic vision; go beyond the numbers of students, attendance zone analysis, and demographic concerns. Establish a planning team that takes pride in the forthcoming facility from a programmatic perspective. Anticipate the need for facility design by a year or two. Allow a minimum of nine months to orchestrate the entire process.

---

* Depending on the space in question, staff and administrators may also have to write specifications, but the chore generally falls in the laps of the teachers.

Construction in Your Future?
Watch For Environmental and Zoning Issues

Your school is gearing up for construction—either a new building or major remodeling of an existing facility. Before serious planning, much less design work, begins on this project, thoroughly check both state and local environmental regulations and zoning requirements.

Of course, no construction project goes off without a hitch. You can count on revisions to the plans, unanticipated expenses, uncooperative weather, and delays in delivering materials. But by ensuring from the outset that the structure you envision will "fit" within this regulatory network, you'll save time, money, and wear-and-tear on everyone involved.

When I&P Academy (our fictional, K–12, coed day school) started planning the expansion of its arts center, this critical step was overlooked. One corner of the addition ran afoul of the town's Marshlands Preservation Act, a fact that didn't come up until the plans were presented to the local zoning board. Efforts to gain an exception proved unsuccessful.

By that time, the architect's drawings were almost completed. Redesign and redrawing cost both time and money. In addition, the legal expenses associated with the exemption attempt were not included in the project budget. Squeezing in those additional costs meant eliminating some "essentials."

On top of that, the changes in plans had to be explained to the school community. Between the article in the school newsletter and the reports on the zoning board meetings in the local newspaper, it was clear that someone just didn't do his homework.

Choosing Your Researcher

Even if you've recently carried out a building project, do your research. Regulations change.

A Board member, your school's attorney, or the project architect may have the expertise to research environmental and zoning issues. This person is responsible for determining which regulations and codes pertain to your planned facility and how they may affect building design. Document these findings and make this information part of your project file.

If your attorney does not handle this research, have him or her double-check the results. Your attorney should also review the architect's contract and ensure that sufficient errors and omissions insurance coverage is in place.

The Research Process

Begin by pulling together basic information about the proposed facility, including:

- the location of the structure in relation to other buildings and features;
- the building's "footprint," i.e., its approximate length, width, and height;
- a brief description of how the facility will be used;
- the number of persons expected to occupy it; and
- parking and delivery needs.

Turn this information over to your researcher, who will investigate, among other things, whether:

- your state or local government has a wetlands protection statute;
- you are bound by laws relating to endangered species;
- your campus is in a flood plain;
- the state has clean- or storm-water management and run-off provisions;
- you are bound by national/local cultural resource protection provisions, such as a historic preservation act;
- density, height, or occupancy restrictions might be placed on your facility; and
- traffic-management requirements apply to your site.

It is better to know up front, for example, whether a water-retention basin is required for flood control and storm-water removal—before the architect puts pencil to paper or fires up the CAD program. There are implications for design of the facility and related support areas and future maintenance costs.

In addition, restrictions on facility height and/or density can force you into another design option, as can minimum setback requirements. And if your town restricts hours and streets for commercial deliveries, you may have trouble receiving supplies at your new facility during normal school hours.

Working With the Zoning Department and Zoning Board

Involve the local zoning department in your project from Day One. Working closely with this department can help grease the wheels for zoning board approval.

The zoning board can be a wild card. Some are well-run, well-informed, and professional; others are partisan and political. A review of the board's decisions over the past year or two can be informative, helping you spot hot issues and stumbling blocks. Armed with this perspective, you can consider your options, make adjustments, and present your project in the best possible light.

When you bring this type of information to the planning process, you greatly improve your chances of completing construction on time and on budget.

Construction Ahead:
An Owner's Representative Protects Your Interests

New construction and major renovation projects rank among the most complex undertakings your school will ever face—and the devil is in the details. Costs escalate, disputes arise, technical decisions loom—who's in your corner? Before you build, assess the benefits of hiring an owner's representative.

The sole responsibility of an owner's representative is to protect the interests of the property holder—in this case, your school—throughout each phase of construction. This professional can offer a combination of experience, knowledge, objectivity, and time that neither you, as School Head, nor others associated with the project is likely to match.

The Job: Oversight and Insight

This advocate can bring an eagle eye and a sharp pencil to the project, battle the endemic cost creep, smooth out myriad rough spots, and help ensure the successful completion of your project. And while you are adding another personnel expense, a highly qualified owner's representative can save you thousands of dollars, which will more than cover the additional fee.

The following three examples demonstrate ways an owner's representative can provide expertise, service, and savings.

- **Review the architect's design and specifications.** The owner's representative can identify areas where an excessively costly approach may have been recommended. Will this additional expense truly provide value to the school, or is it an overpriced "experiment"? Keep in mind that the architect's fee is usually based on a percentage of the cost of the project.
- **Determine the validity of change orders.** Change orders are part of any construction project—no major undertaking goes exactly as planned from start to finish. However, they can also be used by the contractor to make up for a lack of skill at estimating costs.
- **Mediate disputes.** When the HVAC subcontractor claims that the air-handling system cannot be installed exactly as the mechanical engineer has specified, or wants to substitute a system with a different tonnage capacity than specified, you need an objective, educated point-of-view to reach a resolution.

For an extensive list of the skills an owner's representative should bring to your school's project, see the sidebar on the next page.

Who Should—and Shouldn't—Be Considered?

Traditionally, schools have felt they could "assign" the oversight of construction projects to the school's Business Manager or Facility Manager. While both of these administrators should be part of the "design/build" team for your project, appointing either one as the de facto owner's representative ensures that some other area of that person's responsibilities will suffer.

Can the owner's representative come from within the school community? Certainly, although it's a challenge to find a candidate among the members of your Management Team, Board, or parent body who can bring the combination of extensive knowledge and available time to this job.

While the project architect or contractor may imply that he or she can handle this responsibility, an inherent conflict of interest exists. Neither can be expected to wear two hats and serve as an impartial watchdog for both parties. Inevitably, your school comes out on the losing end.

Architectural and construction firms may also provide this service, but avoid hiring one of the unsuccessful applicants for your project. This "runner-up" may not bring the same enthusiasm to the job or have the requisite status with the other key players.

Often, the best choice to fill the role of owner's representative is a fully or semi-retired person with the strong background outlined below. This individual would be likely to have both the requisite skills and the ability to commit large blocks of time on a flexible schedule, based upon the complexity of your project and your estimated timeline.

Qualifications

Just as you followed a well-thought-out protocol to select your architect, give the same careful analysis to hiring the most qualified owner's representative you can find and afford. This individual should have extensive experience in different phases of construction, with a background as either an architect, a construction manager with a construction firm, or a general contractor.

Your representative should also have contacts with local architects and contractors. With anecdotal and firsthand information about the true construction "working conditions" in your community, your owner's representative will help avoid pitfalls that can seriously erode your construction schedule and, thus, your expected occupancy date.

Depending on the extent of the services you expect, you can hire the owner's representative on an hourly basis or set a fee for each phase of the project. As with all other professional arrangements, you should have a letter of agreement or contract, and that document should be reviewed by your school's legal counsel.

Insurance Considerations

Whether you hire an individual architect or a member of a firm as your owner's representative, have your attorney and insurance agent review the certificate of insurance. You want to guarantee that sufficient liability coverage is being provided.

An individual generally will carry less liability insurance than a firm and may not have as wide a range of coverage. At a minimum, you want to be sure that your school is protected should the owner's representative be injured on the project. Check with your insurance agent to see what exposure, if any, you might have under worker's compensation insurance.

As well as a contract, a firm needs to furnish a certificate of insurance naming the school as an additional insured.

If you hire a retired or semiretired architect, then the school takes responsibility for the insurance. The cost of acquiring the coverage would be prohibitive for an individual.

Before you start your next construction project, consider the benefits that hiring an owner's representative can bring. Keep the "devilish details" where they belong—out of your life!

The Owner's Representative Skill Set

Your goal in hiring an owner's representative is to prevent headaches, save time and money, and ensure a successful project. Use the following list as a guide when interviewing and evaluating candidates for this position.

Your school benefits when the owner's representative has the ability to:

- maintain a good working relationship and open lines of communication with all those involved—from your internal project team to your architect, educational specifications consultant (if you use one), and contractor;
- guide your team through design development and evaluation, drawing and specifications review, value engineering, bid analysis, and schedule formulation phases of the project;
- spend the necessary time on-site. Once construction begins, the owner's representative must ensure that the project is proceeding in accordance with contract documents and guard against defects and deficiencies in the work of all the contractors;
- keep the complete construction file up-to-date from start to finish. At the end of the project, you not only want the as-built drawings, but all the operating instructions, warranties, and other documents relating to the various components of your building;
- ensure that the construction is being undertaken in a safe manner. While the school would not be responsible for any job-related accidents, that doesn't eliminate the possibility of negative publicity;
- lead or guide owner review and site (progress) meetings;
- mediate disputes that will inevitably arise on the job;
- monitor the cost of the project and oversee all proposed change orders from inception to resolution. Ideally, the owner's representative should establish a process and approval system and ensure that all parties comply;
- review all progress billings and approve them for payment;
- coordinate the construction with the other day-to-day activities on the campus, especially if the project is undertaken while school is in session. This can include utility shutdowns, traffic movement around the campus, and delivery of materials and equipment to the site;
- ensure that each piece of equipment—boiler, stage lighting, elevators, computerized controls for the HVAC system, etc.—operates as it should, and that your staff is trained on its proper operation and upkeep; and
- assist with the resolution of any claims against warranty for equipment failure.

Reduce Construction Anxiety for Your School's Neighbors

Last night, your school's Board voted to construct a new middle school. As School Head, you face many detailed and time-consuming tasks with this project—including working with architects, engineers, and contractors, and taking part in fundraising. It's also important to make the most of this unparalleled marketing opportunity.

Of course, you want to keep your school's constituencies up to date and excited about the project. That's internal marketing. When you turn your attention to external marketing—your efforts to grab the broader community's attention—pay particular attention to your school's neighbors.

Your school received permission to build a new structure from the local zoning authorities when the campus master plan was approved two years ago. However, it's still essential to consider the impact on and reactions of the local individuals and businesses affected by the project.

You plan to raze the current building and construct a new—and larger—facility in its place. For at least one academic year, modular buildings will house the middle school. Construction vehicles will disrupt traffic on surrounding streets, the noise level will increase, and workers will be on and around the campus every day.

Start interacting with neighbors long before construction gets under way. By letting them know what to expect, you co-opt the rumor mill before it can spread misinformation, create concern, and cause animosity. Anticipate difficult questions and be prepared to answer them. Listen to your neighbors—they may offer information and advice to help you respond to the community's needs and improve the process. Your first step is to assign your marketing group to develop strategies for communicating with neighbors.

Scheduling neighborhood receptions— specifically targeted to local residents, business owners, and representatives of churches, synagogues, and organizations—is a key tactic. The goal of each event is the same—to provide information about the construction and to answer questions.

To maintain an atmosphere of informality and comfort, ask people connected with the school—current and past parents, alumni, Board members, etc.—to hold these events in their homes. To promote discussion, limit participation at each session to no more than 15.

Mail personal invitations, signed both by you, as School Head, and the specific host for each reception. Phone those who do not respond, reiterating the invitation and encouraging attendance. A day or two before the event, have your Administrative Assistant follow up with a reminder telephone call.

Besides you, others present at the sessions will be the Board President, the architect, the contractor (if hired by the meeting dates), and the Administrative Team member whom neighbors should contact with any concerns. Plan to display renderings of the building and a drawing of the master plan, locating the new structure on your campus and within the neighborhood.

The critical information you share at each meeting should include:

- the programmatic enhancements the new building makes possible, and their attendant benefits to the students;
- an estimated time line for the project;
- the routes construction vehicles will take to and from the site;
- efforts to screen the construction from the neighbors to reduce any unsightliness;
- disposal of trash and debris;
- security measures during construction;
- benefits of the project for the community, such as how implementing the master plan eases congestion at dismissal time;
- availability of the new facility for community use (playing fields, meeting room rental, etc.);
- ways to keep them updated on the project (sign on campus, invitations to view construction progress, photos and information on the school website); and
- the name and contact information of the administrator assigned to respond to concerns.

Your school has made strong efforts to maintain exemplary relations with its neighbors. Continue that positive marketing as your new construction gets under way. By allaying their concerns, you will gain their understanding and support, and your school will continue to be viewed as a local asset.

When Does it Make Sense to Hire an Architect?

Architects provide services well beyond developing blueprints. They serve as advisers and problem-solvers, and provide the all-important professional expertise that's often needed to keep a project on track and on budget.

Their skill and experience helps ensure that the project achieves the desired results—translating program needs into facilities that express your school's unique character and mission.

Four distinct circumstances might lead you, as School Head, and your Board to recommend hiring an architect. Note that each calls for different degrees of professional involvement and skill.

Evaluation of the Status Quo

In this instance, the architect's role would be to assess the present use of your current structure(s), as well as any proposed changes. As a result of this process, the school can (1) make the most effective use of existing space, (2) set a realistic long-range budget that takes both immediate and longer-term needs into account, and (3) create a foundation for planning.

The architect will determine the processes that need to be incorporated into the assessment. For example, a facilities condition survey alerts you to the need for specific repairs and renovation. An energy audit identifies ways the school can reduce utilities costs.

As another benefit, the architect can create current-condition drawings to substitute for any "as-built" drawings that are missing from the school's files. While they won't contain all the specifics, they will be detailed. With these documents at your disposal, future plans can be based on the reality of current conditions on your campus—and you won't be flying blind as you pursue your desire to turn "Old Main" into the new Library/Technology Resource Center.

Planning for the Future

One of the goals of the "evaluation of the status quo" is to build a foundation for planning. If your school does not have a campus master plan, the architect will recommend creating this essential document.

The master plan is a long-range projection of what your campus will look like as it develops—where buildings, roadways, parking lots, playing fields, and other items will be located. One of the strongest benefits of this plan is that schools must consider whether they have sufficient land to support their goals—and what action to take if they do not.

The presence of an architect might also play an important role in the long-range planning process itself. For example, the architect might spark a thorough discussion about whether the historic restoration of a specific building is even feasible. Considering the emotional ties that alumni have to some campus structures, you can't risk announcing a renovation project, only to withdraw the idea because it proves to be unrealistic.

Planning and fund raising go hand in hand, and the architect's expertise can also assist you with this part of the process. At I&P Academy, our fictional, K–12 coed day school, one of the outcomes of the long-range planning process was to construct a new fine arts building. In the initial stages of the planning process, the team generated ideas for what the building might look like and what it needed to support. The architect developed initial conceptual drawings that depicted those ideas.

Before putting the capital campaign machinery into operation, the School Head and key development personnel used these drawings as a "test balloon" with potential major donors to gauge their interest in providing support.

Construction with Existing Constraints

Not all renovation or rehabilitation projects require an architect, particularly if the project is relatively straightforward and a Board or staff member has the background and skills to oversee the work. However, even a "simple" renovation can become complex and time-consuming if all factors are not taken into consideration at the outset. The architect's fee can seem like a bargain in the long run.

Schools benefit from an architect's expertise when undertaking major renovation projects such as a mechanical upgrade (installing a new heating plant or chiller) or technological enhancements (computer wiring). In these areas, it's particularly important to plan to meet not only immediate but future needs.

Construction with Minimal Constraints

The design of an entirely new campus, a major campus renewal project, or construction of a separate facility fall into the "minimal constraints" category. A project of this scope requires having a full-service architect on board to handle the considerable detailed work, beginning with the schematic drawings of space and function.

This is another area in which an architect can assist your school in meeting both current and future needs. A building can be constructed in stages, for example. Two stories might be completed as part of the current project, with the third slated to be added as part of the next phase. If the time delay is more than five to seven years, the mechanical drawings may have to be redone. However, the architect can ensure that all the structural elements are in place to support the addition, whenever it is constructed.

Carefully evaluate the complexity of each construction project your school proposes, and consider the expertise and skills an architect can bring to the project. Your goal is to create facilities that express your school's mission, support your program, and, above all, serve your students.

How to Identify the Appropriate Architect for the Job

A poorly designed building can exercise unwanted control over your school's budget and program for years to come. Within a few months after the ribbon-cutting ceremony, the "if only" list starts to grow.

If only the students weren't already cramped for space. If only equipment would fit easily through the doorways. If only there were a little more (or a lot more) storage room. If only the heating bills weren't running 35% over estimates.

When your school undertakes a construction project, hiring a competent architect isn't enough. The School Head and the Board President must develop a review and selection process that ensures finding the appropriate architect for your particular job. This process helps guarantee that:

- your new facility proves to be sound and functional;
- the design enhances the school's image and reflects its unique character;
- the school can operate this structure effectively and efficiently;
- the school's needs, both immediate and longer term, are served;
- the building meets the expectations of donors and other school constituents who committed their skills, time, and energy to the project; and
- the project reaches completion with your construction budget and time frame (and your sanity) intact.

You will rely on this professional to translate your school's unique program needs, character, and mission into "bricks and mortar." To succeed, the architect must know the right questions to ask, ascertain the school's needs (some of which you may not have identified), bring not just technical skills but flexibility and creativity to the process, and guide your school through the planning and construction of the project.

The Selection Committee

When choosing an architect, holding a design competition may suit some schools' needs. However, the scope of most school projects makes a comparative selection process the logical, cost-effective choice.

As the first step, you—the Head/Board President team—appoint your ad hoc Architect Selection Committee.

- Because this is a high-profile endeavor, both the Board and the Management Team should be well represented.
- You may want to include one or two members from the school constituency (parent, alumnus, faculty member) or from the community at large who have expertise to share, an interest in the project, and time to devote. Avoid making appointments for strictly "political" reasons.
- The professionals you've designated to assist with the project, such as an owner's representative and an educational specifications consultant, are also key members of this committee.

The Selection Process

These nine steps provide guidelines for the Selection Committee in carrying out the architect selection process.

1. Determine the basic criteria.

Generally, schools limit their consideration to local and regional architects. However, in major metropolitan areas or for a high-profile school or project, firms with a national reputation may be included as well.

How selective do you want to be? In an ideal world, you would attract a slate of candidates with experience in the private school world and a clear understanding of your school's unique considerations in terms of mission, program, and character. Realistically, however, you may need to include firms that are less specialized.

Focus on each firm's skills and creativity rather than its size or background. Seek out architects with a demonstrated ability to create buildings that go beyond the standard "institutional" look. Do not rule out a firm simply because it is small or has worked primarily with commercial clients. On the other hand, do not assume that a large firm or one that has designed a similar facility for a public school will adapt more easily to your needs.

2. Develop a list of architects for consideration.

Based on their own practical knowledge and suggestions from others, the committee members should be able to identify firms that meet the criteria. In addition, contact other private schools for recommendations based on their direct experience.

Your final slate should include at least six candidates, but no more than nine. This is critical—a longer list will bog down the selection process and unnecessarily delay the overall project.

3. Make an initial inquiry call to each firm to gauge interest in your project.

The Selection Committee should divide the list of candidates among its members and set a deadline for making the contacts. Prepare a simple script; the contact person needs to be able to describe the reason for the call, provide a quick overview of the project, respond to the most likely questions, and stave off requests for more information than the school wants to give out at this point.

Some candidates may "self-select" out of the process. They may be overbooked, unable to work within your time frame, or simply not interested enough in your project to submit a bid.

4. Refine and finalize your list.

If the inquiry calls have resulted in a viable pool of candidates, you're ready to proceed. If too many have been winnowed out, you may need to reconsider some firms that were eliminated earlier.

5. Invite all firms under consideration to a group orientation conference.

Many of the candidates will have the same basic questions; this session allows you to answer them in the most efficient manner.

Provide the candidates with a "rough" scope of the project and the "sketchy" timetable you have in mind. Also distribute background information about the school—your admission brochure, mission statement, enrollment projections, etc. Your goal is to give everyone a clear understanding of the nature and extent of the project.

6. Set a time for each firm to return to the school to make a 30-minute introductory presentation.

These initial proposals can be made to two or three members of the Selection Committee rather than the entire group. Emphasize that this introductory presentation is not an opportunity to describe how the architectural firm will address the school's needs. Instead, it is designed to introduce: the firm, its skills, and its accomplishments;

- the qualifications of the professional staff;
- the firm's experience, if any, in serving private school clients;
- the relationships the firm has with other consulting professionals, such as engineers, who might be involved in the design and construction process; and
- the overall approach the firm would take to managing a project such as yours.

Despite your instructions about the purpose of this session, some architects will gamble and lay out a detailed solution, hoping to sway the majority of the Selection Committee and win the job. This strategy is risky; unless there has been a longstanding relationship, the firm has not had time to develop the empathy with the client that helps ensure a successful outcome.

While you may initially agree with their "take" on the project and appreciate their desire to cut to the chase, do not award extra points for their actions. You may be rewarding risk-taking over architectural talent. Consider whether you would be comfortable undertaking a project with someone who has demonstrated, right from the start, an inability to follow your directions!

You might consider these introductory presentations as a series of "first dates." Based on what you see, hear, and experience in each case, you can determine whether you want to proceed or not.

7. Investigate the qualified candidates and reduce the list to a maximum of five.

Once the firms have "passed" the introductory presentation, further pruning of your list requires contact with references. You want to gauge whether each firm's clients considered their project a success.

The finished buildings aren't the only consideration. You also need feedback on each architect's professionalism, responsiveness, and ability to meet deadlines and budget. When it's practical, a tour of the structure can provide valuable insights as well.

If you know of a previous client who was not listed as a reference, determine why that project was not included.

One or two members of the Selection Committee should also visit the office of each architect to meet the personnel who will be supporting this project. Visual clues about "how they work" and other perceptions gained by talking to the staff are significant and should be given approximately the same weight as client references. While your primary dealings probably will be with the firm's principal members and the project architect, support personnel have a vital role to play in the successful completion of any project.

8. Schedule proposal sessions.

Each finalist should be invited to present a 90-minute proposal to the full Selection Committee. When confirming the day and time of the meeting, send the firm a preliminary description of your project, any educational specifications you have developed, the preliminary budget, a proposed time schedule, and any requirements you have for fundraising materials such as artist's renderings or building models.

Also include a list of all the finalists with the names of the representatives. This tactic brings additional competition into the process and "sharpens the pencils" of each architect when it comes to discussing fees. A caveat: Fees will, of course, be one of the determining factors in your final decision. Beware of figures that seem too low; they may be an indication that the architect will look for corners to cut in order to stay on budget.

Plan to hold these sessions over a one-and-a-half-day sequence. You have undertaken a comparative selection process—to be fair, you need to maintain a tight sequence so that you are in a position to "shop" comparatively. Schedule a break between each session to give the committee members time to process the information and record their impressions.

9. Reach a decision and announce the results.

Once all the presentations have been completed, hold a formal meeting of the committee while the information is fresh in everyone's mind. Generally, if the process has worked effectively, a clear "winner" will emerge with little debate. However, if the committee becomes deadlocked, you may need to gather additional references or data, or develop additional criteria that will inform your decision.

Formalize the decision with a recommendation from the Selection Committee to the Board of Governors. The Board must ratify the selection and the school's legal counsel must review and approve the proposed contractual agreement.

Only then can you contact the selected firm. Once the contract has been signed, personally notify those firms not selected and thank them for their time and interest. If they ask for specifics as to why they were not chosen, provide any information you feel comfortable sharing. Your feedback may help them with future presentations, and it acknowledges the time they have spent on your project.

With the signing of the contract, you should be prepared to release an announcement to your constituents so they can share in the completion of this major step in your new project.

By following a carefully crafted selection protocol, you go a long way toward ensuring that your school selects the appropriate architect—and gains a facility you'll be able to point to with pride as it serves the needs of your program and its students over the years.

How to Handle the 'Pre-selected' Architect Dilemma

Plans are under way for a new fine arts center at I&P Academy, our fictional, K–12 coed day school. Excitement's running high about the first new structure on campus in a decade and, although the architect hasn't been announced, the assignment will go to Fred, of course.

The school has called on Fred's skills in connection with several renovation projects. He was a logical choice—a graduate, a current parent, and a generous and reliable donor to the school's fund-raising efforts. In the minds of many, Fred has been "preselected" for the upcoming project; the school's relationship with him precludes serious consideration of any other architect.

The Board, however, must avoid making assumptions, take an objective look at the situation, and act in the school's best interests. Should this implied relationship continue? Or would the school benefit from spreading the net a bit wider? Perhaps the project requires a firm that specializes in this specific type of structure, or an architect with more extensive skills and experience.

Should the Board determine that the "preselected" architect would not be an appropriate choice, be straightforward. Designate one or two members to advise the individual that he or she will not be considered for this particular project. Explain that, because you value those past efforts, you want to avoid having this person invest time and energy in going through the selection process. Make it clear that this is a special circumstance—you are not precluding this architect from consideration for future projects.

However, if you are willing to consider this candidate, clarify that he or she does not have a "lock" on the upcoming project. Again, one or two Board members should meet with the architect to explain the reasons for opening up the process and to assure that equal consideration will be given to all candidates.

You want to avoid creating a rift. However, you may find that the architect's response is relief. He or she may agree with your assessment that the project exceeds his capabilities. Or the architect may have felt obligated, as a "friend of the school," to take on a project that would require more time than the firm's schedule could comfortably accommodate.

When Holding a Design Competition Makes Sense

The design competition approach to selecting an architect is rarely used by private schools because it adds both time and cost to the project. However, this option may be worth considering if you:

- want to attract architects who might not otherwise consider your project;
- value the regional or national recognition this approach might bring to your school;
- plan a high-profile project (perhaps your campus has historic significance); or
- have a donor who is excited about the competition idea and willing to support the additional cost.

Facilities Projects: Get Organized!

Will you be creating a campus master plan in the near future—or updating one done a few years ago? Are you considering an addition to a building, new construction, or any other facilities-related project on your campus? Hitches and glitches are almost inevitable, but getting organized will hold them to a minimum.

The architects and/or contractors involved in the project can, and will, do a better job for you if you provide them with complete, reliable information about previous projects. This is important in all cases, but especially valuable if they have not worked with your school before.

It's equally important for them to understand the limitations they must work around. To get them up to speed, put together a list of your school's "sacred cows"—the people, places, and things that must not be tampered with in carrying out the project.

Documents

Word-of-mouth information is often incomplete at best and inaccurate at worst—and it can easily be misunderstood or overlooked. Providing the architect or contractor with written information on decisions and requirements that can impact the project helps ensure solid planning right from the start.

Start with a copy of the complete file from the campus master plan process. Information on what decisions were made (and why) is invaluable to those involved with implementing that plan.

If your school does not have a master plan in place, carry out this important step before undertaking a construction project. Rely on an architect or consultant who has experience with private schools to guide you through the process.

The following documents also provide invaluable information to those guiding the project.

- Any land surveys done for previous projects.
- Detailed, as-built drawings, especially those that show the location of the mechanical and electrical systems in each building. If you don't have these documents, contact the architect who designed the project to get a complete set. If CAD (computer-assisted design) software was used, request a copy of the disk(s) as well.
- Documents showing where the underground utilities are placed. A look at these plans will help the architect determine whether lines need to be rerouted (or their capacity expanded) for the new project.
- Any easements your school granted to other property owners, utility companies, or government entities, and any easements granted to you. Provide copies (not the originals) of deeds and other real-estate documents.
- Any special-use conditions placed on your school by the local zoning board. For example, did the city restrict your use of the city streets surrounding your school, thereby limiting parent drop-off and pick-up? Did the city put a time limit on the development of the property? How, if at all, do these conditions impact your new building?
- Existing building ordinances. Do you have letters in your files that need to be passed along concerning, for example, setbacks, the minimum number of off-street parking spaces that must be provided, specific traffic-circulation patterns, or a requirement that a sprinkler system be installed the next time substantial changes occur in your building?
- Existing agreements with your neighbors. Correspondence or, better yet, minutes of meetings with neighborhood associations will alert your architect or contractor to potential issues that may need to be addressed.
- Complete copies of the specifications and bids from your two most recent projects. These are valuable reference documents. If your school wants to maintain certain types of standards—in lighting, bathroom fixtures and appointments, signage, etc.—knowing what was specified previously is a time-saver. You also ensure the same or comparable standards for the new space.

'Sacred Cows'

Sacred cows are those values and priorities that a "stranger" cannot intuit about your school. The architect or contractor needs thorough information about what to watch out for in planning and carrying out the project.

Which of the following pieces of information do you need to provide?

- A list of the "preferences" expressed by your major donors and other key members of the school community. Your school's founder may feel that brick is the only appropriate material for campus buildings. Or these supporters may prefer a classical approach rather than a postmodern design for the new arts center.
- Existing landscaping plans and drawings. The importance of certain campus elements may be obvious to you, but not to an architect. Do not overlook traditions like the path that provides a shortcut between the gym and the playing fields or the memorial trees that were planted by the Class of 1945. If the trees must be eliminated to accommodate the new building, begin now to "soften the blow" for those alums who will be affected by this loss of campus history.
- "Historic building" considerations. As with memorials, your alums, teachers, students, and parents may have strong feelings about the overall look of the campus and the structures on it.

The more information you can provide up-front, the more successful the design phase of the project will be. Your efforts might also save you money: The architect won't have to re-create documents that already exist and will be able to avoid costly errors in design that must then be "fixed" before construction can begin.

If you are just finishing a project, now is the perfect time to start this preparation process. Your job is not over until you gather a full set of design and construction documents so that you're ready for the next undertaking—once you've caught your breath!

Your School's Facilities: Preserve and Enhance Their Unique Character

What does a private school look like? Of course, there's the pervasive image of the New England prep school, with its stone buildings and towering oak trees. But, in fact, private school facilities come in all shapes and sizes. Rarely, however, do they look institutional.

One reason is that many of the buildings were not originally constructed as schools. In addition, one primary characteristic of private schools is their desire to create and maintain a homelike atmosphere.

When you're able to both make the most of your facilities and generate that special home-away-from-home quality, it sets you apart from the public schools in your community. This special character identifies for parents one of the "differences" that makes your school worth the tuition.

Where Private Schools' Character Originated

Private education predated public education in the United States. Wealthy families sent their sons to schools for training, initially, as lawyers, ministers, or doctors. Later, their daughters followed; for them, "finishing school" was the norm.

With the expansion of universal public education, private schools became the alternative. Parents seeking the benefits of advanced academics, smaller class sizes, a select mix of students, single-sex education, and/or a commitment to religious instruction sent their children to private schools.

In these schools, educational philosophy took precedence; facilities were secondary. Private schools started in ordinary homes, in mansions, on estates, and in churches. As private education grew, farms, hospitals, hotels, even strip-mall storefronts were converted into school sites. Some even moved into unused public school buildings. It is only in relatively recent years that private schools have started out in brand-new facilities.

Some of the traditions, unique qualities, and distinguishing characteristics that we see in private schools today stemmed from teachers' and students' "adaptive behavior" as they worked within the limits of their facilities.

Without an auditorium, assemblies and drama productions called for greater creativity. Staging a play with only minimal sets, costumes, and props involved creative risk-taking. Members of the community pitched in to help with the production.

Without state-of-the-art athletic facilities for basketball, wrestling grew into a major winter sport, while cross country dominated the fall or spring line-up. Without extensive science equipment, instructors came up with innovative experiments and projects. Without playground equipment, students relied on their imaginations and the opportunities their campus offered.

The Benefits of a Homelike Atmosphere

The homelike atmosphere that dates from the early days of private schools is one that today's schools should actively preserve—and increase. This "homeyness" is symbolic to parents, indicating a correspondingly homelike level of caring and concern.

Parents want and recognize their child's need for this type of atmosphere. When both parents work, or if the family has been disrupted by divorce or death, this becomes a prime selling point. When "homeyness" abounds in a school, it fosters a more personalized attitude in students and teachers. Even visitors can sense an intimacy and camaraderie that is missing from the public schools.

In this atmosphere, students can be found sitting on the floor by their lockers, reading or quietly talking; a teacher and student may perch on the stairs to chat about a homework assignment. There's an overall feeling that, in this place, people are comfortable, happy, and respectful of each other.

What Gives a School Its Special Character?

A preschooler arrives for her first day. The classroom is lined with colorful bulletin boards and posters. Artwork hangs at her eye level. There are curtains in the windows. A rabbit in one corner begs for attention. She spots a sand table, two activity stations, and the rocking chair the teacher sits in when she reads to the class. There are bean-bag chairs near the bookshelves.

A new seventh-grader comes into his classroom. The desks and chairs are grouped into fours; in his previous school, everything was lined up in rows. Off in a corner, a sofa sits next to shelves overflowing with books. There is also a computer "nook." On the windowsills sit pots of geraniums the teacher grows.

Nooks and crannies should be preserved or created. These out-of-the-way spots provide quiet havens for studying or just relaxing. Propped up against a tree or seated on a bench near a pond is a wonderful way for a student to tackle a drawing assignment or a tough calculus problem.

Over time, it's easy to lose perspective on the effect such simple things as carpeting, plants, paintings, bookshelves, and other personalized touches can have.

Assessing Your School's Character

In the name of convenience, economy, modernization, or conformation to fire codes and governmental regulations, have you standardized too many areas in your school? Are you making continual efforts to maintain and enhance your school's character?

Walk around; analyze your school. What do you find that contributes to its character and uniqueness? What detracts? Ask individual Board members, alumni, parents, teachers, and students to do the same—or form a committee specifically for this purpose. Compare your analysis with the feedback you get from these observers. (See the character-enhancement strategies on the next page.)

Once you've determined where work is needed, assign projects to the most appropriate group or individual, from the Board to the Facilities Manager to the Parent Association.

Environment shapes everyone in your school, affecting their attitudes, performance, and behavior. In sterile, institutional settings, students and teachers stagnate; in an attractive, creative one, they thrive. Strive to retain the atmosphere of those early private schools—a home away from home.

Character-Enhancement Strategies

✓ Take an objective look at how hallways and classrooms are "decorated." Are displays creative and colorful? Do they change frequently, or do they get dog-eared, dusty, and outdated?

✓ If local regulations severely limit what can be placed on your school's walls, talk with the fire marshall about compromises and alternatives.

✓ What about the walls themselves? Are they all painted the same standard, institutional off-white or light green? Yes, your Facilities Manager loves having everything the same shade because it makes touch-ups easy. But aren't there places in your school that would benefit from a little color?

✓ Even if your building started out as a public school or shopping plaza, you can modify that institutional "look." Add a mural, landscaping, and flowers; exhibit student sculpture on the front lawn or walkway; even locate (or relocate) well-maintained, frequently used athletic fields to the front or side of the property where they are visible to passers-by.

✓ Renovate an old building rather than constructing a new one. Look for an architect who has experience in preserving old buildings. Lower the ceilings; improve the lighting; add proper acoustical treatments; install new carpeting or refinish the quarry tile floor; upgrade or add new heating, ventilation, and air conditioning. You'll preserve tradition and create a building that is attractive, functional, and homelike.

✓ In planning a construction project, reject any architect who thinks in "public school" terms. If you're adding a structure, look for someone with experience in designing new buildings that blend with a site's existing character. Or, if you are starting from scratch, choose a creative individual who can work with you on identifying the kind of character you want your new campus to have and making it a reality.

✓ Retain an interior decorator (perhaps a parent volunteer) who can develop a "palette of interior finishes" that is harmonious and compatible with the atmosphere you are trying to maintain. Ban institutional paint colors and ensure that all wall treatments, carpeting, furniture, and other finishes add to the character of your school.

✓ Appoint a "landscaping czar" to coordinate with the Board's Buildings and Grounds (or Facilities) Committee on both exterior and interior plantings at the school. Make sure plants are in abundance year-round. Do not overlook the summer, when last-minute applicants are touring your school. A school that feels like home is easier to market at any time, but it's especially important when your campus is not buzzing with students and teachers.

✓ Empower your Parent Association's Arts Committee to assemble and maintain a revolving art show throughout your school.

✓ Discuss with your Facilities Manager why school character is important. You want this administrator to be an enthusiastic advocate and suggest additional ways to enhance the homelike qualities of your buildings and campus.

Facilities Rentals Yield Benefits—As Long As You Cover Costs

Private schools often benefit from various outside group and organization requests to rent their attractive, well-equipped, well-maintained meeting rooms, gym, theater, and other spaces. While, as a Business Manager or Facilities Manager, you know that there's a nuisance factor connected with rentals, allowing outside groups to use your school's facilities has desirable outcomes.

- There's an opportunity to market your school. Making your facilities available to the community can create increased awareness, build goodwill, and generate positive word-of-mouth.
- Buildings occupied in the evenings and on weekends are less attractive targets for loitering and vandalism.
- Of course, a key consideration for most schools is that rentals can provide a stream of additional income.

However, a school can lose money on rentals if costs are not fully covered. Determine which facilities to rent (to whom and when), and then ensure the financial equation benefits your school.

Base your rental fees on solid financial data rather than using guesswork or making decisions on a case-by-case basis. Review both your rental fee schedule and the actual cost to your school of renting your facilities. Decide on the level of profit, if any, you want to make, and determine whether additional charges are warranted for specific uses or special spaces. Ensure the amount you charge each renter is fair so that, if asked, you can clearly explain how the fees are set.

The following checklist serves as a guide in assessing the range of costs that factor into facilities rentals during the school year—the first step in setting your rental fees. You can use the same approach to determine summer costs and fees for the use of playing fields or grounds.

Refer to the accompanying chart for a look at how I&P Academy, our fictional, K–12 coed day school, figured its basic rental fees.

Rental Coordination and Facilities Operation

Compensation of the Rentals Coordinator who handles your rental enquiries and agreements. If not a full-time job, determine the percentage of the coordinator's time spent on rental-related tasks. Apply that percentage to the person's total compensation (salary and benefits).

Miscellaneous administrative and staff overhead. Other personnel devote time to rental matters. This might include, for example, the receptionist who takes initial phone calls; the office secretary who publishes the calendars; and even you, as the person who schedules facilities personnel and verifies that the renter has proper insurance.

You may decide, for example, to assign a factor of 2% to cover the time the staff devotes to this area and apply it to their total compensation.

Note: I&P Academy chose another option for figuring total administrative costs. An office secretary serves as Rentals Coordinator, in addition to myriad other tasks. The decision was made to allocate her entire salary to the rentals equation rather than figuring percentages for all personnel involved in this area.

Compensation for facilities and security personnel. If rental-related activities tend to result in significant overtime pay for these employees, estimate that amount and add it to the total for regular salary and benefits.

The facilities budget other than personnel, including Provision for Plant Renewal, Repairs, and Special Maintenance (PPRRSM) or depreciation.

Insurance costs that relate directly to facilities and the rental program. For example, does renting your buildings increase the premium for the school's liability insurance?

Furniture and equipment replacement. Make sure to figure in this expense if it is not included in your operating budget. For example, folding chairs and tables will need replacement more often when subjected to the extra wear and tear of rentals.

Other miscellaneous costs. Add up these costs and divide them by the total number of square feet under roof. The quotient is the average cost for operating one square foot of your buildings.

Operating Costs for Rental Spaces

I&P Academy—School-Year Rental Fees

Rentals coordination and facilities operation costs (school year)	
Administration (Rentals Coordinator and other personnel)	$26,500
Facilities and security personnel	$193,450
Facilities budget (other than personnel)	$347,835
Insurance (facilities portion)	$30,000
TOTAL	**$597,785**

Cost per square foot

Total rentals coordination and facilities operation		Square feet under roof		Cost per square foot
$597,785	divided by	125,120	equals	$4.77

Operating cost for rental spaces

Space	Square footage	Cost per square foot	Total
Multipurpose room	2,500	$4.77	$11,925
Gym	15,000	$4.77	$71,550
Theater	10,800	$4.77	$51,516
Meeting room (average)	1,200	$4.77	$5,724
TOTAL			**$140,715**

Rental fee per hour

Total operating cost for rental spaces		Total hours buildings are open		Rental fee per hour
$140,715	divided by	1,440*	equals	$97.72

*180 days x 8 hours per day

Determine the square footage of each space you have available for rent. I&P Academy offers its gym, theater, multipurpose room, and various meeting spaces, including classrooms and the Board room. The school decided that figuring a separate fee for each individual meeting space would be too cumbersome, both initially and in terms of billing and record-keeping. Instead, the school set an average square footage and came up with a single fee for meeting rooms.

Multiply the square footage of each room times the cost per square foot to yield the cost of operating each space during the school year. Add the totals for each room to yield the grand total. (See the chart on the previous page.)

Rental Fee Per Hour

The final step is to divide the grand total by the total number of hours the buildings are open during the school year. The quotient is your per-hour rental fee, the minimum you need to charge to break even.

You can use the per-hour figure as a starting point and adjust rental fees to ensure that the school recoups its costs. For example, your school may want to rent its "basic" spaces—classrooms and meeting rooms—for slightly less than the per-hour rate, as a goodwill gesture. That's fine, as long as you increase the rate for the use of larger, more specialized spaces.

To make the effort on the school's part worthwhile, you should set a two-hour minimum for the use of "basic" spaces and a four-hour minimum for specialized areas like the theater and gym.

At I&P Academy, for example, the hourly rental fee came to $97.72, rounded to a flat $100. The school decided to charge $85 per hour for its smaller rooms and $125 per hour for the gymnasium and theater—a rate that is defensible, given the more specialized nature of the latter spaces. The meeting rooms have high-frequency/short-time use, while the gym and theater have low-frequency/long-time use.

An adjustment might also be required if it is your school's policy not to charge community-service organizations (Scouting groups, the Neighborhood Association) for use of meeting space.

While you can "donate" facility usage and absorb the cost, clearly understand how much you give away—and how often. Is this a public relations/marketing cost? Will that budget cover the wear and tear that results? On the other hand, if all costs must be covered, have all other renters pay a higher fee to subsidize the free users.

There are benefits to facilities rentals—just make sure you understand the "costs." It's worth taking a look at your fee schedule and actual operational expenses. Then, you can determine whether your approach to rentals represents sound fiscal management.

Planning School Grounds for Outdoor Learning

At many private-independent schools, scheduling and space issues continue to frustrate school administrators. Yet, many schools also dedicate time and money to maintaining their campus grounds—space that often lies vacant during much of the school day. Why not take advantage of this available space by creating outdoor classrooms and learning areas?

The Benefits of Outdoor Learning

Many private-independent schools offer annual or semi-annual camping, hiking, or nature trips that help students to better understand the natural world through such activities as investigating wildlife, walking trails, and exploring rock formations. As Head of School or Department Chair, you can work with the faculty to incorporate similar ideas on a smaller scale right on your own grounds.

An outdoor education center can transform a drainage gulch into a lab with an amphitheater and wildlife habitat, including a wildflower meadow and a miniature arboretum with native trees and shrubs. A creek running through the site becomes a wetlands area with a small pond that collects and recirculates water. With proper planning and scheduling, you can bring science and other studies to life.

Creating outdoor spaces such as amphitheaters or covered pavilions and porches for lectures makes good use of space. When equipped with electricity and data ports, these spaces can be utilized more regularly. Students and teachers can use their laptops even when sitting next to a pond on your school grounds. Compared to constructing or renovating buildings for more classroom space, outdoor learning areas can be a less costly option. Even urban schools with little or no grounds can use local parks, marinas, and other public areas.

Schools that work to create outdoor learning environments experience two major benefits.

1. **Outdoor learning areas provide additional teaching space with minimal construction.** As enrollments increase for many schools, it becomes necessary to rethink space and availability of classrooms in an effort to ease scheduling difficulties. While rethinking the building itself may be necessary, it should only be a part of the equation; analyze the space available on your entire school campus. Most likely, your grounds are underused during the school day.*
2. **Well-used outdoor environments offer options that stimulate interest and curiosity.** Research shows that students are better able to absorb and retain math, science, language arts, and other skills when all five senses are engaged.

How to Get Started

Begin by forming a committee that includes you (the Head or Department Chair), key members of the faculty, selected administrators, the Facilities Manager, and any buildings and grounds personnel who will be involved. You may also include the School Nurse for advice on outdoor safety issues. Discuss whether or not the addition of an outdoor learning center would be beneficial—from various perspectives. Draw a large, detailed, and accurate diagram of your grounds to help the committee better understand the size of your property and the current positioning of structures, fencing, and roadways, as well as natural elements such as trees and streams. Your committee should carefully consider the following questions (and others specific to your school).

- What types of learning centers do we want to have, and which areas of the grounds best suit the needs of each?
- What do our grounds already have to offer (soft and hard, wet and dry, quiet and noisy areas, etc.)?
- What is our climate throughout the school year—and how will that affect our plans?
- What can we do to ensure that our outdoor classroom(s) will be beneficial throughout the entire school year—even during cold or wet seasons?
- Who will use the outdoor classroom(s) and when?
- Who will build the outdoor classroom(s) (volunteers or a professional team)?
- What kinds of safety precautions should be made for students (e.g., protection from long-term exposure to UV rays, removal of any poisonous plants, insect repellent to ward off mosquitoes)?
- What sort of maintenance will our plans require, and who will be responsible?

Of course, it is critical to understand what the final costs will be before you begin the project. Keep in mind that volunteer labor and donated materials can play a tremendous role in your project's success.

Involving your students in the assessment of existing school grounds and in proposing ideas for their use is an excellent way to solicit feedback and instill pride in the results. Promote the project in your school newsletter, on the Web site, and during assemblies to encourage enthusiasm and commitment on the part of everyone—staff, parents, and students.

Take the time to visit schools that have successfully implemented outdoor learning into their curriculum. This will aid you in the decision-making process, particularly because you can learn from their mistakes and successes.

Once you've decided to implement an outdoor learning program, you'll need someone to spearhead the project. The most successful programs assign responsibility to an individual (often a motivated member of the faculty) to coordinate the effort. This person's understanding of gardens, animals, wildlife, etc., enables him or her to assist the school in best utilizing its property—or other public areas of land that may surround the school. Teachers go to this coordinator for assistance with lesson plans, ideas, and suggestions to design innovative and enjoyable ways they can take their lessons outdoors.

Creative Ways to Move Outdoors

Consider some of these inventive ways to create outdoor learning environments with minimal expense.

- Refurbish an unused barn to create a mini-nature center.
- Place a cluster of picnic tables under a wooden canopy to create a group meeting area, which can double as an outdoor cafeteria.

- Build a sandpit and include large tree stumps or flat boulders as seats for a conversation area.
- Add enclosed gazebos with benches or chairs and a blackboard to create an outdoor traditional classroom.
- Develop mini-ecosystems where students can learn about wildlife. Wildflower gardens, toad homes, butterfly gardens, hummingbird feeders, bird baths, wetlands, a barn for domesticated farm animals, and amphibian pools are just some examples.

To Find Out More

To learn more about outdoor learning environments, start by contacting:

- your state Department of Natural Resources or state wildlife agency;
- the North American Association for Environmental Education, a professional network of educators that provides publications and grants. Visit the association's Website at: **www.naaee.org**; and
- a landscape architecture and planning firm in your region with creative experience in school campus design.

---

[1] ISM has long taught that, to maximize space efficiency, classrooms should be occupied throughout at least 80% of the school day. Why not apply the same rule to your grounds as well?

Classroom Acoustics and Learning

On any given day, according to the American Medical Association, 18% of the U.S. student population suffers from mild hearing loss caused by congestion or ear infections. Add to that number the more than 8% of American children who have what is termed an "educationally significant hearing loss," and a clear challenge arises: How do you, as the Facilities Manager, ensure that your school classrooms facilitate students who have trouble hearing what their teachers are saying?

Noise from heating and ventilation systems, students in adjacent rooms, and the exterior (e.g., lawnmowers, airplanes, traffic) are the norm in most classrooms. Poor reverberation, or how much sound is echoed in a room, can also create distracting background noise. A teacher may raise his or her voice to compensate, but this can be fatiguing and irksome for both the teacher and the students.

Other teachers may opt for amplification. However, many acoustical engineers say that microphones do not address the critical problem. "Wearing microphones is a solution if using crutches is a solution to broken legs," says David Lubman, an acoustical consultant in California. "When classrooms are reverberant, amplification doesn't help. It makes it louder, but not clearer."

Are Acoustics Really a Problem?

Studies continue to show that classrooms can be a hard place in which to listen. University of Florida acoustics professor Gary Siebein visited 26 schools and about 600 classrooms, and discovered that 50% of the students who sat behind the first two rows in these classrooms could not understand their teacher.

A University of Kansas analysis also found that the speech intelligibility rating in most U.S. schools is 75% or less—meaning that listeners with normal hearing could only understand 75% of the spoken words.

Though poor acoustic conditions can detrimentally affect any student's learning process, certain students are especially at risk:

– ESL students who require more favorable conditions for understanding classroom conversations. Missing just one word per sentence can lead to complete confusion.

– Young students—those less sophisticated listeners who can't "shut out" background noise as well as older children and adults. (Children's ability to understand sentences in noise improves through the early childhood years, reaching adult performance levels during the teen years.)

– Students with minimal hearing loss. Fifteen percent of students aged six to 19 studied by the Centers for Disease Control and Prevention in Atlanta had a hearing loss of at least 16 decibels (16dB to 25dB is considered slight/ minimal loss).

– Students who suffer from recurring otitis media, or ear infections. OM is the most common medical diagnosis for young children.

– Students with attention deficits who already struggle to remain focused during class discussions.

Do not wait for students to report difficulty hearing. Schools must be proactive. Most children (and adults, for that matter) may not know they have "misheard" a message unless they have already had experience with the language and the topic under discussion. Children frequently have an unrealistic perception of the amount and accuracy of the information they are receiving. Therefore, even if a teacher asks, "Can you hear me?" the child will usually say, "Yes." A child cannot estimate the quality or quantity of information that he or she did not hear in the first place.

How to Improve Classroom Acoustics

Of course, there is no comprehensive set of criteria that will yield "good acoustics" for all rooms and uses. Your school may have small classrooms, large lecture rooms, auditoriums, music rooms, cafeterias, and gymnasiums—each with different acoustical requirements. In order to understand how these different spaces should be designed, you must first familiarize yourself with the basic properties of sound.

Even armed with knowledge of sound and design principles, however, you are not an expert. The best course of action is to call on the services of a professional acoustical consultant who can fully evaluate your school and make suggestions for improvement—most of which need not be exorbitantly expensive.

The following list suggests easy and often inexpensive changes that can make a world of difference in the classroom.

- Carpet classrooms to quiet feet, books, chairs, etc.
- Put acoustic tile on the ceiling and an acoustic treatment on the walls.
- Use landscaping that muffles external noise.
- Provide concrete barriers between traffic and classrooms.
- Put sound absorbing material in the space above the walls between classrooms.
- Use acoustic ceiling tile and carpet in the hallways.
- Line heating/cooling ducts with acoustic materials or baffles.
- Seal cracks between rooms and on outside walls.
- Use doors that have mass (not hollow-core).
- Back permanently mounted chalkboards or bulletin boards with sound absorbing materials.
- Use double wall or thick wall construction. Add additional layers of gypsum board, plywood, or other construction material.
- Hang thick curtains or acoustically treated blinds.
- Place rubber pads or carpet under noisy equipment.
- Encourage children to wear soft-soled shoes.
- Place some form of rubber tips on the legs of desks and chairs.
- Place flat surfaces at an angle to reduce sound reflection.
- Turn off computers when not in use.
- Place pictures on bare walls to help absorb sound.
- Have humming fluorescent lights replaced.
- Install curtains in front of shelving units.

No school, even a new one, should feel exempt from possible classroom acoustic problems. Many older schools have noisy heating and ventilation systems; cracks in walls, which allow noise to pass through easily; or inadequate windows that permit considerable sound transmission from outside. Though these problems may not exist in newer schools, such buildings were likely constructed with thinner, more lightweight materials (which provide little noise reduction) rather than the heavy brick and concrete block used 50 years ago. In addition, many schools built in the 1960s and '70s were designed with open-plan classrooms, that have since been permanently partitioned—but noise reduction between rooms may still be insufficient.

As you refurbish school facilities this summer, take measures to ensure that you provide quiet classrooms that foster learning and development (rather than headaches and confusion).

Streamline Your Housekeeping Services

As Business Manager or Facilities Manager, you know that providing housekeeping services is not just about "cleaning"; it's about how people are motivated to serve "customers." The challenge for administrators is to provide consistent and continuing leadership to these employees, enabling them to deliver excellent service on a daily basis, while keeping an eye on the bottom line. If no one has communicated your housekeeping standards, the multiple desires, needs, and expectations in your school community can create confusion and misunderstanding on the part of both your housekeeping staff and their "customers"—your school's Board, faculty and staff, parents, and students.

The keys to maximizing the effectiveness of the housekeeping staff (whether you outsource or not) are to:

- determine the "goals" for your housekeeping services;
- define the services that will (and will not) be provided by your housekeepers;
- once you've set the goals and the services to be provided, disseminate that information to your housekeeping staff and everyone else in the school community;
- provide continual training for your housekeepers to enable them to meet or exceed your goals;
- commit to providing quality equipment and supplies that allow employees to do the job as expected; and
- establish a plan to improve the compensation of those housekeepers (if you do not outsource) who meet and consistently exceed your expectations.

There are two driving factors in setting the standards for your housekeeping services: ensuring the health and safety of everyone in your community and making your school an attractive place in which to work and learn. Also, don't overlook the role facilities play in marketing your school. Facilities are tiebreakers when a family is making the decision to attend—as well as stay in—your school.

Perform a Housekeeping Audit

As the first step in maximizing these services, conduct a housekeeping audit designed to measure the current level of expected performance against the actual level achieved. This audit will establish the goals for your housekeeping services and serve as a planning document for weekly, monthly, quarterly, semiannual, and annual cleaning tasks. All areas of your school should receive focused attention at least annually—and more often as necessary. A simple matrix can be developed to account for all the areas of your school. (See the accompanying chart, "I&P Academy: Housekeeping Audit," on page 65.) For each specific area, the audit should cover the:

- degree of use and population impact each day (occupancy density);
- number and types of rooms and spaces to be cleaned;
- frequency of use per week;
- types of floor coverings, walls, and ceilings in your facility; and
- cleaning frequency desired.

Score each area of your school using the scale found in the chart.

Different areas will require different degrees of attention. Determine the level of excellence you require for each, and devise the strategies required to achieve and maintain it. For example, bathrooms should receive a high score (they require daily cleaning), but your Business Office may only need to be cleaned every other night. You may decide that your Admission Office needs to be cleaned daily because it is highly visible to visitors, but the auditorium can be cleaned once every two or three days (if it is only used minimally on a daily basis).

The weather in your area will also influence your audit. Frequent rain or snow will require different attention than drier, milder climates. You will need to adjust work schedules and loads from season to season to achieve excellence.

Next, assess the skills and levels of competence of your housekeeping staff. Where do your personnel excel; where do they need additional training or support? Where do they complement one another; where are they disparate? For example, you may have no one on your staff with skills or training in maintaining tile floors, although over 65% of your school's floors are tiled! Keeping tile in shape is quite different from working with carpeted floors.

With answers to these skill-and-competence questions, you'll have a head start in knowing the skills you seek in new employees when staff vacancies occur. The audit also will highlight where you need to provide additional training for current staff. Alternatively, you may decide to supplement your cleaning staff with an outside contractor to take care of jobs for which you have neither the expertise nor the equipment.

Communication and Training

Once you have completed your audit, devise your communication and work/training plans to meet your goals. Your housekeeping personnel need to be aware of who their customers are, and your customers need to know what services to expect and in what ways they will be provided.

Housekeeping services can cause headaches for everyone if service goals (and levels of excellence) have not been communicated to your constituencies, faculty and staff in particular. Simply saying the housekeepers clean the facility each night gives little direction to the housekeeping staff and is not a measurable goal. The definition of "cleaned" is left to each individual in the school community to interpret.

Communication is done best by:

- having regular meetings (at least once per week) with your housekeeping staff, highlighting both the areas that meet your expectations and those that do not. Such meetings can also provide an opportunity for "mini-training sessions" on a cleaning technique or product usage; and
- at least once a year, including housekeeping services as an agenda item for your faculty and staff meetings. This gives you an opportunity to "educate" all employees about your goals and objectives and to refresh everyone's memory about the duties of the housekeeping staff. During this session, review what these employees do and explain how to request special services. Take time to point out tasks that are not part of the housekeepers' duties and responsibilities. Faculty

and staff may not understand that a burned-out light bulb is handled by your maintenance crew, not the housekeeping staff. If there are seasonal fluctuations in the duties, (e.g., snow removal), then a universal (email) memo when the seasons change is one way to remind everyone about the shift in emphasis.

Do not overlook involving your faculty and staff in achieving excellence in the housekeeping department. For example, you could require teachers to have the students place all the chairs in their rooms on top of the desks each night, making it more efficient for the custodian to vacuum a classroom. Or, the last class of the day in a middle or upper school room might be asked to pick up all stray papers and other trash from the floors. Teach students that they are responsible for picking up after themselves. With an investment of teacher and student time, more efficient use of your housekeeping staff's time will surely be one of the outcomes. Additionally, your students will be showing that they respect the work done by your housekeeping workers.

Encourage teachers and students to write "notes of appreciation" for the services provided. Housekeepers often work behind the scenes and have minimal interaction with the students, so it is more difficult for them to feel that the work they do impacts the classroom and the whole school community.

If your budget permits, provide uniforms for the housekeeping staff. This will promote recognition, and it becomes a "benefit" to the employees, since they will not have to buy work clothes. Wearing a uniform bearing the school's name, logo, and the staff member's name instills pride and commitment. If your resources permit, consider providing laundry services as well to ensure "uniform" neatness among the entire staff.

Establish an evaluation system that is "growth" based. Work with your housekeeping staff to determine what skills need to be acquired and what problems each individual needs to solve. Base your "raises" on achieving those skills or solving problems. Basing compensation only on inflation or across-the-board increases provides minimal incentive and does not reward excellence.

Invite your housekeepers to school activities such as sports events, concerts, and banquets—make them feel like a part of the school community. If the housekeeping staff has contributed above and beyond, special recognition might be in order. A pizza party or cookout, to which their families are also invited, is a nice way to recognize excellent work and show how appreciative you are of your employees. By taking a proactive approach, you endorse the fact that quality housekeeping service plays an important role in the educational environment your school wants to provide and gives the custodian "pride of ownership" in his or her work.

I&P Academy: Housekeeping Audit

Type	Room Area #	Occupancy Density	Times Used	Flooring Type	Frequency Desired	Excellence Desired
Dining Area	100	5	5	5	5	20
Kitchen	100	5	5	5	5	20
Bathroom-Boys	212	5	5	5	5	20
Bathroom-Girls	214	5	5	5	5	20
Health Office	225	5	5	5	5	20
Gym Changing Rooms	320	5	5	5	5	20
Admission Office	130	5	5	1	5	16
Head of School	170	5	5	1	5	16
Hallways	—	5	5	1	5	16
Gymnasium	300	4	4	3	3	15
Art Room	280	5	3	5	2	15
Science	260	4	4	5	2	15
Lower School Office	210	4	5	1	5	15
Grade 1 Room	230	4	5	1	4	14
Grade 2 Room	232	4	5	1	4	14
Grade 3 Room	234	4	5	1	4	14
Grade 4 Room	236	4	5	1	4	14
Grade 5 Room	238	4	5	1	4	14
Faculty Lounge	250	5	5	1	3	14
Library	150	3	5	1	3	12
Music Room	270	3	5	1	3	12
Computer Lab	290	3	5	1	3	12
Business Office	140	3	5	1	2	11
Development Office	160	3	5	1	2	11
Assembly Hall	200	3	3	1	3	10
Board Room	190	2	1	1	1	5

Use a scale of 1 to 5 (1 exhibits a low concern/frequency/priority; 5 exhibits a high concern/frequency/priority).

Definitions:

Occupancy Density: 1 equals low, minimal use by few people; 5 equals high, maximum use daily by a large portion of the school community.

Times Used: 1 equals infrequent use (average week); 5 equals daily use or a "high profile" area that needs daily attention.

Flooring Type: 1 equals flooring (usually carpeting) generally deemed easiest to clean; 5 equals flooring generally deemed hardest to keep clean. Type of flooring and its usage and location in the school will influence your rating. Carpeting at the school entry will need attention every day; carpeting in the Board Room requires less attention.

Frequency Desired: 1 equals a low priority; 5 equals highest priority.

Excellence Desired: This is the sum of the four ratings (occupancy density, times used, flooring type, and cleaning frequency desired) to help set priorities. 1–5 equals minimal level of excellence desired; 6–10, low level; 11–15, average; 16–20, high level. Each school determines its own levels of excellence in the spaces it uses and maintains.

Common Restroom Problems and Student Health

According to a Kimberly-Clark Professional survey conducted by Opinion Research Corporation, 20% of middle and high school students admit to completely avoiding school restrooms because the facilities are dirty and unsanitary. A similar study concerning public restrooms, by Impulse Research for the Georgia-Pacific Corporation, determined that, of those surveyed:

– 80% are worried about germs in restrooms,
– 40% flush the toilet with their feet,
– 60% don't sit on or touch anything, and
– 30% completely avoid restrooms because of hygiene concerns.

Keeping school restrooms clean, safe, and well functioning can be a tremendous challenge for Facilities Managers—and is a primary janitorial/housekeeping expense. Though keeping restrooms in top shape can be a daunting task, it is extremely important. Unclean restrooms lead to two main health threats: the spread of germs, and infections and other conditions that result from retaining urine to avoid using a public facility.

1. Unclean restrooms are havens for harmful bacteria.

Dr. Charles E. Gerba, a microbiologist at the University of Arizona, Tucson, has found playgrounds and classrooms to be full of invisible microbes such as staphylococcus, E. coli, and coliform. Restrooms can be a breeding ground for such microbes. Consider: After using a public restroom, a single hand can have a bacteria population of 200 million, according to The Centers for Disease Control (CDC).

The CDC reports that hand washing is one of the "most important means of preventing the spread of infection." However, if restrooms are not well stocked, students can't keep clean. For example, if soap dispensers are not filled consistently, even students who have made hand washing a habit cannot properly do so. Students then carry these germs all over your school.

2. Waiting can be dangerous.

Unwelcoming bathrooms (i.e., restrooms that are dim and dingy; lack supplies, like toilet paper and soap; or have broken toilets and sinks) leave students feeling that they have no other choice but to wait until they get home. This is dangerous for a child's health.

Dr. Michael E. Mitchell, professor-in-chief of pediatricurology at Children's Hospital in Seattle, WA, frequently sees children, especially girls, with bladder and kidney infections because they refuse to urinate in school restrooms. Some develop a persistent inability to empty their bladders properly. To avoid this problem, schools must work to create restrooms that students feel comfortable enough to use on a regular basis.

Restroom Odor

Even schools that clean their restrooms regularly can run into odor problems. For example, officials at one university searched in vain for the source of a stale smell in their facilities. Officials were surprised to find the ceilings glowing yellow under a black light. As toilets are flushed, they disperse an aerosolized mist of bowl water and urine into the air that frequently lands on the ceiling. In time, the build-up is strong enough to cause an odor.

Understanding the conditions that cause odor helps Facilities Managers devise strategies for successful removal. The most common causes of restroom odor include poor cleaning that fosters bacterial growth, inadequate ventilation, unflushed fixtures, and failure to service floor-drain traps. Also, the warmer the temperature and higher the humidity, the greater the likelihood that a restroom will smell.

However, in most restrooms, the odor is caused by bacteria using urine as a food source. As the bacteria grow, so does the odor. Bodily fluids that feed bacteria are often found on the interior, exterior, and underside of sinks, urinals, and toilets.

Another frequently overlooked source of odor is the floor drain. If the trap dries out, it emits sewer gas. Cleaning crews should pour a cup of water down the drain each month to keep the trap full and stop the gas from escaping. Adding enzymes or pouring a capful of vegetable oil down the trap also helps seal in the gas and keep the trap from drying out and causing odor.

Getting it Clean

- *Disinfect restrooms daily.* Housekeeping crews should use an acid neutralizer to remove urine from floors. Grout, including floor and wall grout, is a perfect place for bacteria to grow, so pay close attention to these areas. Enzymes digest the bacteria's food source, as well as the bacteria itself, causing the bacteria to die. Do not use enzymes in conjunction with disinfectants that can destroy the enzymes before they are able to digest the bacteria.

- *Use proper cleaning techniques.* Proper mopping involves two steps: applying cleaning/disinfecting solution liberally to the floor for 10 minutes of wet contact, then removing the soiled solution. Disinfectants need 10 minutes of "dwell time" to kill bacteria. Use adhering-foam disinfectant cleaners for vertical surfaces.

- *Deodorize.* In restrooms where poor airflow is a problem, a deodorizer can be mopped in or sprayed into the air. Some are time-released or come in blocks that are attached behind toilets. Many are made from glycol, which makes the odor molecules heavier than the surrounding air, causing them to fall to the ground where they are later removed by cleaning. The key is to eliminate the source of the odor, then clean the contaminated area. The last step is to deodorize.

- *Conduct thorough and regular restroom inspections.* Begin in the hall. How does the entrance look? Well-lit and inviting? Inside, use your senses. Touch the walls: Are they scummy? Scan the room: Any graffiti? Anything broken or leaking? Are paper towel and soap dispensers full? Listen and smell: Is the ventilation system working?

- *Regularly inspect restrooms with an ultraviolet light.* Body fluids (e.g., urine, blood, and saliva) contain phosphorus and glow under a black light. Note the locations, or mark areas needing cleaning with a UV (invisible) ink pen. The special ink glows in UV light and can be removed with water or cleaning solution. In follow-up inspections, you will be able to see which areas have not been cleaned.

- *Create a flow chart sequencing tasks.* The Facilities Manager should post the chart in the janitorial closet or behind the restroom door, then provide hands-on training to ensure workers form correct work habits. An organized cleaning cart with a specific place for each item saves time and makes replenishing supplies easier.

What's Working Well for Schools Today?
- Many schools have installed sensor-triggered toilets, sinks, and lights to reduce odors and conserve resources. The mechanics are on the inside and not easily broken.
- At I&P Academy, the boys' and girls' restrooms are connected with a vestibule of wash stations for students of both sexes to share. This allows for maximum student supervision. In lower schools, this also cuts down on children playing in the sinks. In middle and upper schools, this thwarts vandalism, smoking, and other problematic activities. This design also lends itself to doorless entryways, which enhances ventilation and cuts down on the spreading of germs on doorknobs.

As Facilities Manager, consider ways to improve the sanitation and use of your school's restrooms, and enhance student hygiene and safety in the process. Even minor changes in the layout of restrooms, such as installing sensor-operated toilets and sinks, can make a difference.

Your School's Indoor Air Quality: Is It Hazardous?

When schools conduct their regular risk management audits, they need to look beyond the obvious environmental problems of radon leaks and asbestos. For the past few years, the Environmental Protection Agency (EPA) has named indoor air pollution as one of the top five environmental health risks.

- EPA studies indicate that indoor levels of pollutants may be two to five times, and occasionally more than 100 times, higher than outdoor levels.
- People spend an average of 90% of their time indoors, increasing their exposure to indoor pollutants.
- The American Lung Association says asthma cases have tripled from the early 1980s.

Although all buildings should be evaluated for their indoor air quality (IAQ), schools must be especially vigilant as children can be particularly susceptible to indoor pollutants. They have smaller lungs and are, thus, breathing in a higher ratio of pollutants relative to their size. Furthermore, they are often more active and congregate in large numbers in small rooms. Schools need to assess their levels of indoor air pollution and take measures to eliminate or reduce it.

Why Worry About Poor IAQ

In 1994, the Massachusetts Department of Motor Vehicles moved from a drafty old building to a new high-rise. Within six months, more than 50% of the employees were sick—many quit. Officials traced the problem to cheap ceiling tiles that, while serving as a ventilation plenum, were also fermenting! The building is now closed, and litigation is proceeding.

Indoor contaminants can have many detrimental effects on the occupants and the building itself. Poor IAQ, including variations in temperature and humidity as well as airborne contaminants, can cause premature deterioration of the physical plant; decreased performance levels in faculty, staff, and students; and health difficulties, ranging from increased susceptibility to common illnesses to Sick Building Syndrome (SBS).

SBS's symptoms are lethargy; headache, dizziness, and nausea; irritation of mucous membranes; and sensitivity to odors. The key to recognizing SBS is that the symptoms appear when the person enters the room/building and disappear when he or she leaves. However, SBS is only one illness associated with indoor pollution. People may experience reactions when exposed to combustion products, biological contaminants, heavy metals, or volatile organics. Your school's health professionals should be aware of and keep logs detailing symptoms that could help diagnose an IAQ problem in the school.

The Causes of and the Solutions for Poor IAQ

1. Inadequate ventilation

A secretary at a public high school in Vermont quit her job after a year-and-a-half, attributing her migraines, nausea, vomiting, and colds to poor IAQ. Tests found higher than acceptable levels of carbon dioxide in the classrooms, indicating poor air circulation and ventilation. Subsequent tests revealed the lingering presence of benzene and styrene, which are commonly found in cleaning compounds. The school district estimates it will cost $1.5 million to install a new heating and cooling system.

School buildings erected before the 1960s are drafty enough to take care of most ventilation problems. Early 20th century standards called for 15 cubic feet per minute (cfm) of outside air for each occupant, primarily to dilute and remove body odors. However, in order to conserve energy during the 1973 oil embargo, the circulation of outdoor air was reduced to only five cfm per occupant. In many cases, this measure was found to be inadequate to maintain health and comfort. In 1989, the American Society of Heating, Refrigerating, and Air-Conditioning Engineers revised its standards back to 15 cfm in most spaces and 20 cfm in offices. If your school has buildings constructed in the '70s or '80s, or remodeled during those years, the ventilation is probably insufficient. Check with your state for local building regulations.

Solutions: Start with your heating, ventilation, and air-conditioning (HVAC) system—schedule periodic cleanings and filter replacement, and make sure it is operating at capacity. It's possible that deferred maintenance, the most frequent cause of poor IAQ, or neglect has caused a deterioration of air-handling effectiveness. If you have rooms served by "univents," make sure no one has stacked books or materials on top of the vents or blocked the bottom intake vents.

In older buildings without HVAC systems, installation of all-building fans in the attic will draw fresh air into the building. Where there are strong pollutant sources (e.g. restrooms), increase local exhaust ventilation and vent it to the outside.

2. Chemical contaminants from indoor sources

As part of its building renovation, the EPA installed new carpet. Shortly thereafter, 60 people became sick and 10 had to be hospitalized. The fault was toxic levels of chemicals in the carpet.

Most indoor air pollution comes from sources inside the building. Although many are aware of the hazards associated with lead paints and varnishes found in older buildings and furniture, they may not know that adhesives, carpeting, manufactured wood products, copy machines, pesticides, and cleaning agents may emit volatile organic compounds (VOCs) (e.g., formaldehyde). At high concentrations, VOCs can cause chronic and acute health effects.

Further VOC contributors are tobacco smoke and combustion products, which produce respirable particulate matter as well. Combustion products include emissions from furnaces, space heaters, and water heaters. At the aforementioned high school, concentrations of carbon monoxide were found in the wing containing the auto shop.

Solutions: Well-ventilated facilities are your best defense. Install exhaust fans in high-contaminant areas, and vent the source emissions to the outside. Ban any tobacco smoking in the building. Store and use paints, adhesives, solvents, and pesticides in well-ventilated areas, and use them during periods of nonoccupancy. Don't overlook art and science storage areas as sources of pollution. Allow time for building materials in new or remodeled areas to air out before occupancy.

3. Chemical contaminants from outdoor sources

Ironically, an air-delivery system can be a source of indoor pollution. Pollutants from motor vehicle exhausts, storage sheds, plumbing vents, and building exhausts can enter the building through intake vents and windows. If pesticides are sprayed near an open window or the air-conditioning intake vents, the chemicals can enter the ventilation system.

Solutions: Don't allow school buses or cars to idle their engines near your fresh-air intakes. Move dumpsters away from the building, and make sure any organic materials are properly sealed in plastic bags. Do any outside maintenance involving chemicals on the weekends or during the summer; allow time to vent whatever compounds enter the building.

4. Biological contaminants

In January of this year, a private school in Seattle was closed for the testing and elimination of health-threatening fungi (including stachybotrys) that were found in ceiling tiles. Airborne stachybotrys can cause chronic migraines, dizziness, stomachaches, and respiratory problems.

Bacteria, molds, microbes, and viruses breed in stagnant water in ducts, humidifiers, drain pans, or anyplace where water has collected (e.g., ceiling tiles, carpeting, or insulation). Insect droppings from an unchecked infestation, animal dander, and pollen are also pollution sources.

Solutions: Make sure animal habitats in your school are properly cleaned and aired. Place floor mats at the building entrances to prevent contaminants from spreading throughout the school. The next time it rains, carefully survey the building for leaks and puddles to indicate areas that may contribute to microbe growth. In areas where water may collect, such as in front of drinking fountains, use removable and washable area rugs. Vacuum the carpets on a regular basis with a high-filtration vacuum cleaner.

Take baseline readings of temperature, humidity, and chemicals to find out what your building is like when it's healthy, so that you have markers for monitoring changes. Educate your faculty and staff about possible signs of poor IAQ, set up a team to investigate complaints, and have an IAQ plan prepared in case of emergency. Education, communication, and a thorough knowledge of your building are your best weapons against indoor pollution.

Teams Keep an Eye on Campus Safety

In the past, summer provided the perfect opportunity for a thorough school safety check—quiet campus, empty buildings. Today's campus is in almost year-round use, so that down time is now packed with everything from summer camps and sports team practices to new-family picnics and property rentals.

While you still need a major once-a-year safety review, periodic checks make sense. Form a Safety Team made up of members from various constituent groups in your school. Each will bring a different set of eyes to the process.

In addition to the Business Manager and Facilities Manager, you might include your janitor, a teacher from each division, parents and grandparents, a Board member, and students. Also involve a first-responder (police officer or firefighter) and a neighbor (a resident or business-person) who might see after-hours activity on your grounds.

From season to season, shift the members so they are inspecting areas that are not familiar to them. For example, the Athletic Director might check the chemistry lab and a grandparent might be assigned to the cafeteria.

It's also a good idea to set up a "Sweeps Team" to conduct a daily check of the buildings and grounds. (See the sidebar.)

These precautions are important, but they are not stand-alones. They will only be effective as part of an overall risk management/crisis planning protocol.

The Safety Team in Action

Arm your team members with a basic checklist to fill out as they go. The completed checklists are turned in to the Facilities Manager, who reviews the items and areas that need attention and creates an action plan to address them.

No checklist can cover every possible safety concern, but there are a handful of "must haves." These seven facilities hazards are the ones ISM identifies most frequently during an on-site Risk Management Analysis.

- **"Sharps" on playground equipment**
  A close inspection may reveal jagged pieces on the equipment itself or protruding from the ground. Look from various angles—for example, underneath benches or equipment where adults wouldn't go, but children would. Change of seasons, aging, and enthusiastic use can cause these "sharps," which can be responsible for minor and major injuries.
- **Inadequate cushioning in "fall zones" on playgrounds**
  The recommended level of cushioning is six to 12 inches. Do you still have a reasonable amount, or has it been walked off?
- **Issues with bleacher maintenance, policy, and practice**
  – Are outside bleachers in good repair?
  – Are retractable bleachers in good working order? Do you have a strict and well-understood operation policy for the bleachers? Do you keep the key in a safe place and away from unauthorized users?
- **Unsafe school traffic patterns and management**
  – Do you have a clear traffic flow for pick-up and drop-off?
  – Are traffic cones, zebra stripes, and speed bumps used effectively?

Sweep Team

The Sweeps Team is charged with a morning "safety sweep" of the campus. Its mission is to be certain that the premises are safe to enter for the school day. If possible, a sweep should also be conducted at the end of the day.

This group is a subset of the schoolwide Safety Team, made up of three to five members. Set up a rotation system—with the membership changing monthly or quarterly—so this task doesn't become a burden.

This team performs "rounds" each morning, about 30 minutes prior to the arrival of parents and students. They are looking for anything amiss, and specifically checking for the following items.

- Open windows and doors
- Broken glass
- Unlocked gates
- Items thrown onto the playground overnight
- Cars parked on or near the campus that are not recognized
- Proper operation of the security card system (if any)
- Nothing is blocking any hallways or points of egress (exits)
- Any rooms presenting special hazards (janitor's closet, boiler room, labs, shops, etc.) are locked
- Anything else out of the ordinary that should be checked to ensure student safety

If there are significant safety concerns—such as a broken window or forced door—that could indicate a possible intruder on-site, team members should not investigate on their own, but rather call 911 or the police.

- Do you have sufficient supervision to control students as they enter and exit the building?
- Do parents create dangerous situations by trying to "short-cut" the system?

- **Hazardous conditions in the janitor's closet**
  All too often, this storage area violates every rule of common sense. Potentially poisonous cleaning solvents are easily accessible. Flammable items have collected in a corner. A fuse box is tucked away behind a hodgepodge of equipment. Neither a sprinkler nor a smoke alarm is installed.
- **Unsafe storage in the boiler room**
  – Are there flammables near an ignition source?
  – Are hazardous substances kept well away from heat and in a locked closet or container?
  – Is the shut-off switch well marked? Is it accessible, or has it been blocked with school detritus?
- **Hidden science lab hazards**
  Your school no doubt has the requisite safety precautions in place. Are they being implemented?
  – Does the equipment (e.g., fire extinguishers and eyewashes) actually work?
  – Are goggles available and in use?
  – Has the first-aid kit been checked to make sure it's well stocked and none of the contents are out of date?

– Are emergency procedures clearly posted?
– Do your teachers review these procedures each year?

As you set up your schoolwide and sweeps teams and conduct safety reviews, keep parents informed. You might put a short article in the newsletter or incorporate this information in a Head's Letter. There's no need to report every inspection or every finding; your goal is to reinforce for parents that you demonstrate an ongoing concern for their children's safety and are taking specific actions.

Checklist Identifies Steps to Improve Security on Your Campus

A safety check is part of the process of preparing for each new school year—whether it's your job as School Head, or a responsibility you assign to the Business Manager or Facilities Manager. Before the teachers and kids walk back through the doors, you want to make sure to fix the loose railing, replace the leaky pipe, and patch the cement walkway.

Safety is one element—security is another. Replacing a broken window may address both. But how long has it been since you conducted an overall assessment of your campus specifically from a security point of view?

The checklist on the following page gives you the basic security elements to investigate, both inside and outside your buildings. Each school will have different needs. Use the checklist to assess the level of security you desire.

Check off an item only after you've determined that all components are satisfactory. Note deficiencies and, as time and funds permit, address them.

You may want to involve representatives of one or more constituencies in this process. The President of the Parents Association, for example, may spot details that a senior faculty member overlooks, and vice versa. A comparison of the survey results can prove enlightening and helps ensure that you've covered all the bases.

Once you've determined which areas of the school property need attention, work with the Business Manager and/or Facilities Manager to prioritize the projects and take steps to remedy deficiencies. Set deadlines, then follow up to determine that the work has been completed in keeping with the agreed-upon standards.

Use your school's newsletter—and special bulletins, if needed—to inform your school community about the survey findings and any action you have taken or plan to take as a result. Demonstrate that an ongoing program is in place to ensure that the school's people and property are safe and secure.

This list, while comprehensive, is not designed to cover all school situations and configurations. You may wish to seek the services your local police department, an insurance agent, or a security professional if you have major concerns or want guidance on additional ways you can make your property more secure.

Providing a "safe haven" is a top priority, in the eyes of both the families who choose your school and the personnel you employ. Conduct an ongoing assessment as a tool for maintaining security on your campus.

Security Checklist

Exterior Security

Doors
- ❏ All doors are in good operating condition
- ❏ All doors are attached to solid two-inch by four-inch wood or quarter-inch steel frames, which in turn are attached to wall studs
- ❏ All door hinges are equipped with nonremovable pins
- ❏ All locking mechanisms are in good working order
- ❏ All keys (metal and electronic) can be accounted for
- ❏ The school has been re-keyed within the last five years
- ❏ All outswing pedestrian doors are protected with UL-approved latchguards
- ❏ All unnecessary handles, knobs, etc. have been removed from exterior doors not used for entrance/exit
- ❏ A system is in place to ensure that all doors are locked every night

Windows
- ❏ All windows are securely anchored in solid wood or metal frames
- ❏ A system is in place to ensure that all windows are locked every night
- ❏ To prevent break-ins, all first-floor windows are secured with polycarbonate glazing attached by through-the-frame screws, or have comparable glazing

Other Means of Ingress
- ❏ All other openings, such as roof hatches, skylights, air shafts, vents, etc., that are not in use are permanently secured
- ❏ If used occasionally, these openings are affixed with grates or padlocks and hasps

Other Areas
- ❏ All outside areas are well-maintained
- ❏ Trees and shrubbery are well-trimmed and do not provide hiding places
- ❏ There is no trash and graffiti on the school grounds, which indicates a high level of attention to detail concerning your school's grounds and structures
- ❏ All outbuildings are locked
- ❏ Keys for outbuildings are in the care and custody of the Facilities Department
- ❏ All parking areas are clearly marked
- ❏ All lighting is sufficient around building entrances and windows to allow discernment of an intruder from at least 20 feet by the average person
- ❏ Lighting in other outdoor areas—athletic fields, parking lots, etc.—is sufficient to alleviate shadows and allow recognition of shapes and colors
- ❏ The loading dock area is separate from school/community parking; doors are often left open as deliveries occur, which could allow an intruder to slip in
- ❏ The dock's access door is secured when not in use
- ❏ The trash-bin area is secured
- ❏ The trash-bin area is situated far enough away from school buildings to keep the bins from being used as a ladder to gain access

Interior Security

Classroom and Office Areas
- ❏ All classroom and office areas are secured by at least a hollow-core door
- ❏ All have a deadbolt lock or an electronic key or card system
- ❏ All interior lighting is sufficient at all hours in all areas of the facility to deny concealment of intruders
- ❏ All areas have ready access to an emergency-response system, such as fire "pull" station or a cell phone to call 911
- ❏ All lobbies and reception areas—as well as any other areas within the school buildings where visitors or other non-employees gather—are monitored at all times during the hours of school operation
- ❏ All non-employees—visitors, workmen, etc.—sign in upon entering the building and wear a visitor's badge clearly identifying them to the school community

Special Use Areas
- ❏ All areas such as auditoriums, athletic buildings, etc., are open only when a responsible adult is present
- ❏ All such areas are secured in the same way as other school buildings
- ❏ All such areas have a separate emergency-response system in place
- ❏ All such areas are locked in the appropriate manner when not in use

Establish a 'Key' Policy/Security System

Even if your school has the budget for security guards, sophisticated alarm systems, and electronic access doors,* there are other steps every school can take to deter would-be thieves. Many problems stem from the fact that there are numerous keys to offices and classrooms floating around with only an informal system of tracking them. Faculty members often lend keys to upper school students who are using school facilities after hours or during the weekends. Children of employees may also present security problems.

Develop a Key Policy

To prevent unauthorized use of school keys, establish a policy that stipulates regulations and consequences of misuse for faculty or staff members who share keys. Students should rarely have a need for office or classroom keys. If they need to get into any rooms, advise them to have a teacher unlock the door or suggest they sign out a key for a specific length of time. Make sure this policy is understood by all students, faculty, and staff.

If you know there are keys that are unaccounted for or missing, you must rein them in or totally re-key the school. One way to persuade students to turn in unauthorized keys is to announce your key policy at a student assembly; then designate an "amnesty box" where keys can be returned without penalty. After an amnesty period, any students found with an unauthorized school key will suffer the full consequences—perhaps a three-day suspension.

Devise a Key Security System

While no one likes to think of members of the school as security risks, an organized key system can remove temptation. If your school is experiencing security problems, it may be best to re-key everything and start anew by establishing the following recommendations. Even if your school is fairly secure, these ideas should be implemented.

- The Business Manager or Facilities Manager should maintain a master key cabinet containing duplicates of all the keys used in the school buildings, perhaps color-coded for easy reference (blue for classrooms, green for offices, etc.).
- For effective key control and storage, also install key cabinets in designated areas of the campus; e.g., all keys for the Athletics Department could be stored in a cabinet in the Athletic Director's office. The custodial crew, groundskeepers, and other facilities employees then would not need to carry huge key rings. By using key cabinets in various school departments, you can control the number of keys available throughout the buildings and provide better security because only certain responsible people have access to the key cabinets.
- Label all keys so that their functions are clear. Key chains with areas for labeling are available. Keys should be marked "do not duplicate."
- Maintain an inventory of keys—a written list of those who have keys and why.
- Appoint one person to be responsible for control of all keys. This ensures that all information about the whereabouts of keys will be accurate.
- If someone needs to borrow a key, use a check-out system similar to that used by a library.
- Don't give out master keys to everyone on the maintenance staff. Only supervisory personnel should have masters.
- Collect all keys during vacation periods, when employees go on leave, and when they leave your school's employ. In addition to increased security, this measure also reduces the chances of keys being lost. Make special arrangements for your teachers who want regular and easy access to their classrooms during vacations—many of them look forward to vacations as a time to catch up, to reorganize or redecorate their rooms, to prepare special projects, etc. Make it a simple matter for these individuals to arrange in advance to have access to their rooms.
- If a building or wing was recently constructed, be sure to recover all keys used by the contractor.
- Perform routine "key audits" to make sure that everyone can produce the keys they were issued. This ensures that people understand and take seriously their role in security.

With these measures in place, faculty, students, and parents may have to forego some comforts and conveniences to ensure campus safety and security. For example, the high school student who arrives late to school is unable to enter the building through the convenient (but now locked) parking lot door. But, for your key policies and other safety procedures to be perceived as fair and consistent, the entire school community must be convinced of the importance of campus security.

---

* Electronic key systems are ideal in school environments, allowing you to easily reprogram locks and deactivate cards when necessary. While many schools have these "swipe" devices, many do not because of the expense—and even those that do typically still have key systems as well for certain buildings and facilities.

Facilities and Faculty Retention

When discussing ways to enhance faculty recruitment and retention, do you include the condition of your school facilities in your considerations? As Head, if you've noticed teachers complaining about their classroom space, noise levels, air quality, lighting, and other facility inadequacies, this may be a red flag indicating deeper problems.

A 2002 study, *Public School Facilities and Teaching: Washington, DC and Chicago*, implies that correcting poor facilities is essential to attracting and retaining high-quality teachers. Although the study involved surveying public school teachers, the findings have implications for private-independent schools as well. (See the accompanying table, "Facility Conditions: Faculty Satisfaction/Success.")

Over 40% of the teachers cited lack of classroom space—and many reported teaching in nonclassroom spaces such as hallways and even closets. Science labs, music/art rooms, and physical education facilities in particular were considered woefully inadequate. The teachers also felt that their schools provided little or no professional workspace.

Many teachers reported suffering health problems related to their school facilities, with indoor air quality leading the list. Environmental problems result in reduced teacher effectiveness and lost teaching time due to illness (e.g., asthma, respiratory problems, sinus infections).

The study found that poor facility conditions affect faculty career decisions. Among teachers who graded their school facilities with a C or below, more than 40% said they are considering changing schools, and 30% are considering leaving the teaching profession altogether. For teachers who have experienced health problems caused by "hazardous" facilities, the percentages are even higher (50% in Chicago and 65% in Washington are considering changing schools; 40% in both cities are thinking about leaving the profession).

As you analyze your teacher turnover rate, be sure to include your facilities in your evaluation.

Facility Conditions: Faculty Satisfaction/Success		
	Faculty Who Cited the Problem	
	Chicago	Washington
Facility Problems		
Classroom wrong size	44%	42%
Room is not a classroom	27%	27%
Science labs inadequate	56%	64%
Music/art rooms inadequate	39%	50%
Physical education facilities inadequate	28%	44%
No professional workspace	33%	28%
Health Problems		
Bad indoor air quality	55%	68%
Too noisy	44%	68%
Uncomfortable temperature	32%	42%
Bad lighting	10%	22%

Faculty, Facilities, and Technology

Private-independent schools have struggled with integrating technology into buildings for many years now, facing issues such as bandwidth and power sources. Planning our school buildings now requires a deeper conversation that includes teachers. While some schools continue to eschew the greater use of technology for philosophical reasons, most schools that embrace and integrate the use of new technology have a competitive edge in the education landscape. This does not imply that technology is necessarily an attractant. More fundamentally, the power of personalized, adaptive technology and feedback enhances instruction and learning, and can be a game changer in the effectiveness of the school's mission delivery.

Consider the following examples.

- A science teacher at Sacred Heart Cathedral Preparatory School in San Francisco uses a sophisticated version of teaching with various platforms, apps, and modalities. Significant general evidence indicates that this integration of technology improves results, improves satisfaction, and enables more students to achieve higher success.
- At Clintondale High School, MI, a school of choice with a high failure rate, the use of technology licenses and software, the school's website, and YouTube provided access to learning across a spectrum of locations. This resulted in a flipped classroom model, increasing personal face time with students fourfold and reducing the failure rate by 33%.
- At Kalinag Higher Secondary School, Sunkhani Dolakha, Nepal, technology and its integration into facilities planning and education delivery is transforming the potential of a region in every part of their everyday life. It connects faculty as a learning community and connects students to knowledge and learning. The point of this example is to recognize that education is now global and that what happens elsewhere competes with what happens here.

The inescapable conclusion is that the notions of "campus" and "education" are transforming—teachers must be integral to the thinking behind new and re-imagined uses of facilities. There are three ways of helpful thinking (among surely others).

1. There is—and will be increased demand for—flexibility. Much has been written about the inflexibility of the double-loaded corridor, the lecture theater, and the computer and language lab as learning platforms. Teachers and schools committed to personalized learning (teaching each student rather than teaching each class) need facilities to mirror and support their pedagogies and interactions. For example, can all three eighth grade sections watch a presentation, split into varied (by interest) groups to discuss what they have seen, and then go into their "classes" for writing assignments and peer review? What kind of room(s) can support constant change in engagement methods tied to learning outcomes that emphasize depth of learning, disparate points of view, and personal achievement? The traditional 20th century corridor is an illustration of the contrast. A corridor represents the need for transition and typically takes up to 20% of the conventional school. It assumes inflexible organizational structures and learning defined by space, not by real people. Flexible space, on the other hand, emphasizes such concepts as:

- "event space" (places where multiple kinds of activities can take places);
- "lighter building" (buildings where the external skin is rigid and the internal structures can be changed as needed);
- "learning commons" (learning areas controlled by a group of students and a group of faculty); and
- "learning streets" (where every space becomes a learning space, including windows, and corridors).

2. The fall of an empire is slow but sure. The postsecondary level is leading the way in promoting interdisciplinary conversation and even interdisciplinary organization. The school must surely follow suit, given a child's predilection for the unity—not the fragmenting—of knowledge. This complicates issues of control of shared use, access, and responsibility. For example, the Spanish teacher in the lower school may intrude on the homeroom teacher by coming into her room. In the upper school, teachers and departments want control of their own teaching spaces. There are, of course, practical reasons for this desire. However, learning is never at the center of the rationale. The fall of an empire does not imply the collapse of "discipline" or the loss of autonomy. It implies the need for deep faculty conversations about the relationship of their teaching space to student learning space and needs. What new forms are needed to satisfy new ways of looking at content and process, including interdisciplinary learning?

3. The network of physical objects that contain embedded technology (to communicate and sense or interact with their internal states or the external environment) continues to advance. Practical uses include the ability to identify excellent or poor use of space, and ways to optimize. This may involve determining there are not enough conference rooms, or identifying rooms used inefficiently that can result in function changes. Increasing technology use also means that spaces have increasing technology requirements. Can class sessions be recorded for students who are absent to view online, for review, for self-reflection, and for formative evaluation? Is the music practice room set up for the pianist to practice with an orchestra or the trumpet player to perform with the brass band? Is technology an assumption or still an add-on? Teachers grapple with these questions and with their implications for learning and teaching.

Teachers are routinely involved in the advice and counsel part of planning and renovating buildings. However, it is still rare to consider facilities within the context of the broader learning and teaching conversation and within the context of technology use. We recommend:

- beginning capital campaigns for facilities with a year of conversation with faculty about the means and ends of education, with practical outcomes about how space and learning interact with the faculty as the mediator of the space. "We need another science lab" is not good cause for a $10 million campaign to put in four traditional labs and four classrooms. Consider the potential of teaching and learning science over the 25–30 years of that building's existence;
- making the strategic academic plan a prerequisite document before facility change is decided; and

– considering the campus master development plan (CMDP) as a planning document far more complex than most we now see.[4] It is not merely the picture of where everything needs to be when the campus is fully developed, which is certainly good. But the accompanying CMDP document must include also the why, the implications of technological development, the environmental connections between the artificial and natural, and understanding the campus itself as a complex learning environment.

Facilities are "only" the outcome of an interdisciplinary conversation where faculty members argue about how the school's mission must and should be delivered over the next decade. View facilities planning that reflect the past with suspicion; facilities not rooted in the every-day should be viewed with skepticism. When millions of dollars are at stake and the next 20–30 years of education are about to be nailed down, suspicion and skepticism are great places to start.

Facilities Management for the Year-Round School

While schools continue to consider the year-round school in their academic programs, you, as Business Manager, know that schools are already operating 50+ weeks of the year. The resulting lack of down time makes it difficult to carry out ongoing maintenance, significant repair tasks, deep cleaning, adaptation, renovation, and construction (inside buildings, on building exteriors, and outside around the campus on athletic facilities). Yet, the fiscal and parental demands for ongoing use of the facility are not going away.

Managing staff under these circumstances is much more complex. Clearly, you cannot directly supervise all your employees all the time, which leads to delegation of duties and more difficulty in establishing accountability. Even where tasks such as janitorial or transportation are outsourced, your responsibility for their effective completion does not go away. Many schools, small and large, often have too few resources for the expectations laid upon them. The last recession also made clear that the facilities budget is one of the first scrutinized when a school is short of money.

Research findings, while still tentative, are becoming more robust in defining the connection between the quality of facilities and student performance and satisfaction. In one study, the researcher found that, "Not surprisingly, investments in teacher compensation (human capital) and instructional support (social capital) demonstrated larger effects than investments in school infrastructure (physical capital), but all were statistically significant, and hence all are necessary to enhance student achievement." It is important that you, as the Business Manager, understand that your work, as it concerns school facilities, is not just about safety, but about the excellence of mission delivery at your school.

The following questions can help to form the basis for making your school's plant management more mission effective, task efficient, and strategically directed.

- How well do your facilities enable faculty to deliver the school's mission? What does that mean?
- How well is your summer program integrated into the year-round understanding of the school and its facilities?
- Is your school making the right investment in its existing buildings, infrastructure, and academic programs, recognizing not only initial capital costs but ongoing operating costs?
- Is facilities management reflected in the school's strategic and strategic financial plan?
- Is it appropriately funded through the PPRRSM account (part of ISM's cash reserves) at 5%–8% of operating expenses, depending on your deferred maintenance requirements?
- How efficiently do your facilities operate?
- What is the lifetime cost of your facilities?
- How do your facilities operations compare to your peer institutions?
- Are students satisfied with the spaces that you provide?
- Are faculty, staff, coaches, administration, and parents satisfied with the spaces and services that you provide?
- Are you developing your own staff such that they can sustain excellence?

Consider the following strategies.

1. If you have a student body of 450 or more, hire a Facilities Manager (reporting to the Business Manager) not as a worker/mechanic, but as a manager, scheduler, and planner. A year-round school requires intensive planning and scheduling. This role will examine every work order; estimate urgency, time, and costs; schedule jobs to be completed efficiently; and ensure that all materials are on-site when a job gets under way. There can be savings of up to 30% in work-hours when projects are estimated and scheduled systematically. For schools that are smaller, the above tasks are even more important to maximize tight budgets and limited personnel. Ensure that, on a part-time basis, there is a member of the facilities team with the skills and time to carry out this function.

2. Ensure that you have an up-to-date facilities audit and work with your School Head to inform the Board of Trustees about its critical role in ensuring safety, excellence in programmatic delivery, and student performance and satisfaction.

3. Based on the facilities audit and a master list of regularly scheduled maintenance activities, design a yearly maintenance calendar that is updated every three months. This coordinated master calendar must have all programs represented, including:
   - the regular school year,
   - extended day services,
   - summer/vacation programs,
   - parent education programs, and
   - community programs including rentals/leases.

   The calendar should project at least twelve months into the future and should be explicit about the next two months. (See the accompanying graph as an example.)

4. Translate the calendar into a solid work-order system (computerized or manual) for requesting work. Without a clear, well-enforced scheduling system, staff will respond to requests for service as they are made. Once a set of proper procedures has been established, the number of last-minute requests will be reduced. The work-order system will help you devote only as much personnel to a particular job as that job requires, saving time and money.

5. Be sure that your system allows appropriate timing of jobs and tracks job completion. Carefully estimate the time, the amount and cost of materials, and the labor for each job. Then, compare those figures with the actual figures at the end of the job to ensure that you are estimating properly. This will help fine-tune your work system.

6. Track each job from the work request to job completion. Account for every employee and evaluate his or her work on each request submitted. Collect information on the time and cost for the maintenance of your facilities—on a weekly, monthly, quarterly, and annual basis. Use the system to train not just your own staff but the plant users (the adults who want work done).

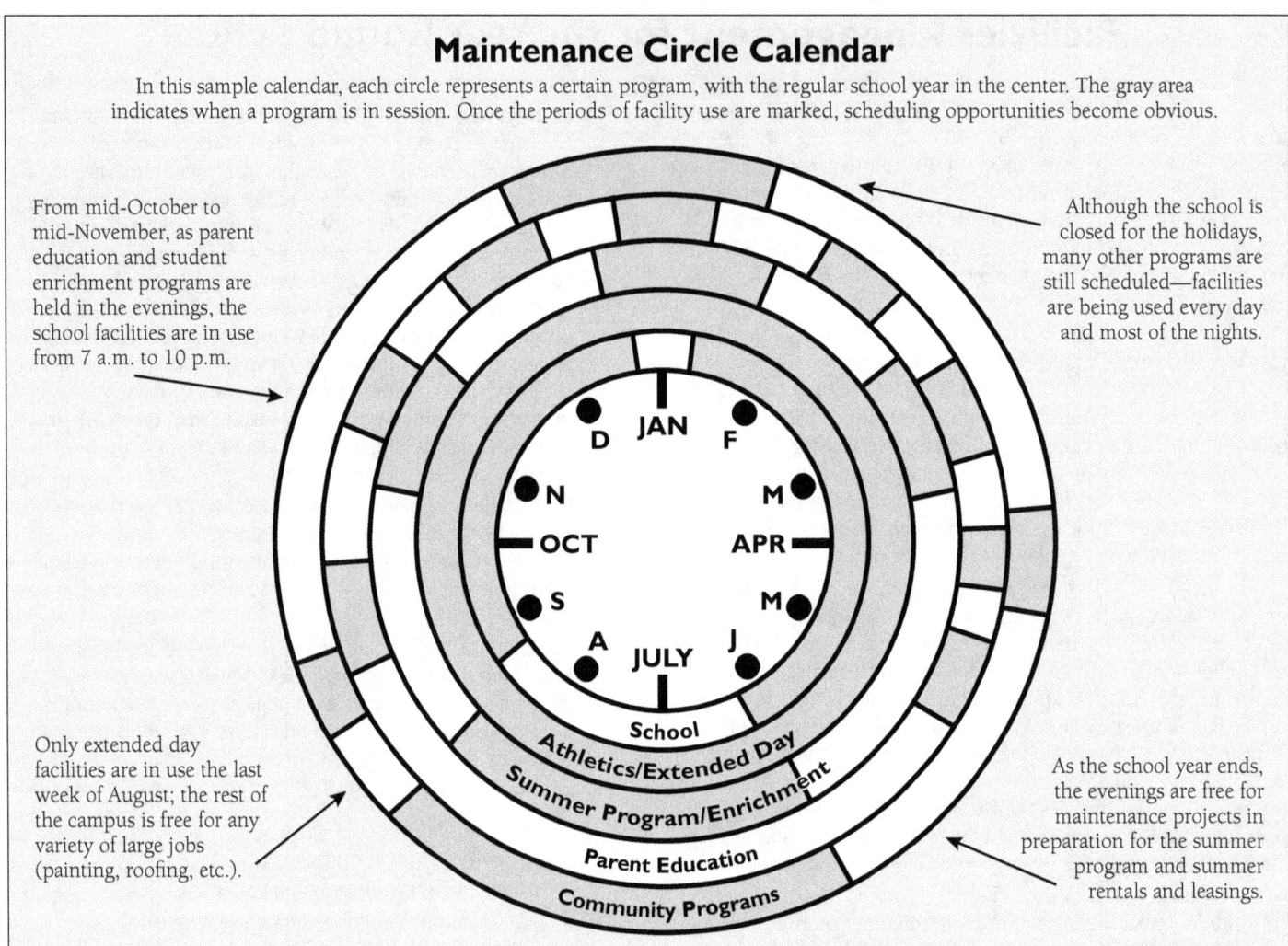

Maintenance Circle Calendar

In this sample calendar, each circle represents a certain program, with the regular school year in the center. The gray area indicates when a program is in session. Once the periods of facility use are marked, scheduling opportunities become obvious.

From mid-October to mid-November, as parent education and student enrichment programs are held in the evenings, the school facilities are in use from 7 a.m. to 10 p.m.

Although the school is closed for the holidays, many other programs are still scheduled—facilities are being used every day and most of the nights.

Only extended day facilities are in use the last week of August; the rest of the campus is free for any variety of large jobs (painting, roofing, etc.).

As the school year ends, the evenings are free for maintenance projects in preparation for the summer program and summer rentals and leasings.

7. The system should also provide key data for accurate budgeting that is based on the needs of the facilities rather than the exigencies of economics.
8. Contract services are helpful when the arrangement is more economical than providing the service in-house (e.g. when a large project would require excessive overtime from your staff), when the job is highly specialized or technical, or occurs on a seasonal or irregular basis. This is particularly important when the window for tasks is a month or less and you have to scale up the scope of activity significantly for a short period of time.
9. Evaluate the true costs of rentals, leases, and summer programming to establish their efficiency value to the school (dollars, time, personnel). Ensure that intentional communication with the Summer Program Director occurs immediately at the end of the current year's program to assess and then plan forward for the following year.
10. Invest in your staff through professional development, including on-the-job training, Webinars, and courses. Ensure that their experiences include seeing the building from the user's point of view—students first, then faculty, other staff, and administration. Develop a student-centered approach to facilities.

Understanding your facilities as a year-round management task allows you to organize your resources more effectively, educate the School Head and Management Team realistically, and maximize student performance and satisfaction.

www.ingramcontent.com/pod-product-compliance
Lightning Source LLC
Chambersburg PA
CBHW060518300426
44112CB00017B/2715